life after death

A Personal Journey of Loss
& a Guide to Navigating Grief

Meaghan A. Hughes

Be a Light Media
Ortley Beach, New Jersey

Paperback ISBN: 979-8-9954981-0-0
Ebook ISBN: 979-8-9954981-1-7

Cover and book design by Jess LaGreca Steidl, Mayfly book design

Library of Congress Catalog Number: 2026908248
First Printing: 2026

dedication

To Jay, Shane, and Emily,
Your love gave me the fuel to write my story.
You three are the great loves of my life.
I know my grief does not just impact me, but all of you as well.
Thank you for your patience, unwavering support and
encouragement, and for lending me the confidence
I needed to believe I could do this.
My love for all of you is eternal and my gratitude is infinite.
XOXO

contents

introduction

Do you ever feel like you can hear your thoughts becoming crystal clear while taking a shower? Maybe it's the way the water seemingly cleanses my mind, or maybe it's just the quiet calm that allows my breath to get deeper and release an exaggerated exhale. *Ahhhhh.* Either way, I've had many of these deep-thought shower moments. Is it God? Is it my intuition? Is it my mother trying to send me a message from up above? I guess I will never know for sure, but on February 14, 2023, while taking a shower, I heard—inaudibly—a very clear message . . .

"You need to write a book about your grief."

Then I heard, *"It will be called Life After Death."*

I was immediately overwhelmed by the message because it was not just a fleeting thought, nor was it something I had been actively thinking about. It was Valentine's Day for goodness sake, writing a book about death was not exactly a romantic idea. But almost intuitively, I also knew it was not just a suggestion. I jumped out of the shower, threw on my robe, grabbed my phone and opened a blank note. Within two minutes I had outlined ten chapter titles. I then put down my phone and took a step back in a mix of shock and awe.

I had experienced the "nudge" before, knowing that I was meant to, or *supposed* to, do something else, something *more*. That nudge was persistent for several years, finally quieting in my mind when I went back to school to begin my master's degree in counseling at age 38. This was different, though. And I knew at that moment that writing this book might be the hardest, as well as the most therapeutic, challenge I would ever experience. Well, challenge accepted.

I had allowed all the self-doubt to creep in too many times. Avoidance had become my bestie. Somehow, after writing had initially come to me effortlessly, I became stuck, avoiding it at all costs. *I think I need to reorganize my closet first and clean out the kids' old toys. We should really donate some of these things.* Then I would warmly welcome imposter syndrome. *You can't write a book! Who will read it? What are you thinking?* We say such nice things to ourselves when we are scared, don't we?! But despite the self-deprecation, I finally decided I'd do it anyway, even if I never published it. So here it is, and if you are reading this today, I somehow miraculously pulled it off.

prologue

Grief comes in many forms . . . grief over what was lost, grief over what will never be again, and grief over what could have been in the future. My thoughts raced after my mom died tragically. *We (myself and my siblings) could not live without her. My mom will never know my future husband. My mom will never know my future children.* Those thoughts, and so many more, consumed me and literally gutted me to the core.

Although much of my own story is death-related grief, grief can encompass so much more. People experience grief from infertility, divorce, job loss, moving to a new town, releasing old friendships, children growing up and moving out, missing the parts of ones' past self, etc. It is not one-size-fits-all.

In my work as a counselor, I have witnessed grief through the eyes of many for a wide variety of reasons, and what I've learned is that grief is hard, it is painful, and sometimes it's terrifying. I have also learned that our relationship with grief will change and evolve, time and time again.

Let me be very clear, this book is not a cure for grief. In the beginning of my own grief, I craved a "cure" because living with it was unbearable. Couldn't someone just tell me how to stop the pain? The simple answer was always "no". But I learned that grief also wouldn't hurt that intensely forever. At times, it washes over us like a tsunami, and other times it is a duller, yet constant backdrop. The truth is, our grief is our genuine love for, and connection to, the ones who have died, and so in that way, I do not want it to ever fully end. After more than 25 years and counting, I'm almost certain that it never will.

This book is a story of my own personal losses, and my slow return to reality over and over again. I have learned that sometimes we need to sit in our grief alone, in the shower, in our bed, driving in our car, in church, or even just behind our sunglasses (thank God for shades!). Sometimes we need to cry, and sometimes we need to scream. Other times we just need to be still. I have also learned that leaning on the people in our lives who entered this godforsaken space long before we did, can help cushion our fall. They have unknowingly paved the way, showing us a glimmer of hope, and that we too can somehow survive this devastation.

We all experience grief on our own timelines, and although it does not end, it most certainly will change. I want you to know that if you can't close your eyes at night because the pain is so great, I've been there. How is it that life is just supposed to resume like normal after loss? It cannot possibly be the same ever again. Yet others, even those who care deeply, seem to carry on all around us. Grief is not visible, so we ourselves may even appear to others like we are okay. For a very long time my grief was ubiquitous. In fact, whenever I was in the depths of my grief, I felt unrelatable to so many around me. All the things I used to enjoy and care about seemed superficial at best. I wanted to take a pause from life and check out for a while. I dreaded small talk and the awkward conversations that inevitably made others feel uncomfortable and made me feel like I needed to comfort them in return. When you feel this dark and sad on the inside, you start to lose hope that your true, authentic self will ever return.

My hope is that this book brings you some level of comfort and to let you know that you are not alone. I also hope that it brings you to a place where you choose to live again.

What happened to my family is tragic and sad, and at times, absolutely beautiful. But this story is *my* journey. My family shares in this grief, but we all experience it differently. There are as many versions to this story as there are people who experienced it, and while each family member is a huge part of my life, I am not here to tell their stories. My pain and loss have led me to live my most authentic life. I would not be who I am today without it. My grief is a significant part of me, it is not *all* of me. But it is, without a doubt, intrinsically woven into the fiber of my being.

June 1999, my high school graduation and our last picture as a family of 7
Left to Right: Brendan, Daddy, Gail Katherine, Me, Kerry, Brian and Mommy

PART I

stuck in the dark

CHAPTER ONE

the worst day of my life

In August of 1999, at the age of 18, I was ecstatic about starting my college career at the University of Scranton in Scranton, Pennsylvania. Growing up at the Jersey Shore, I knew that I could never live too far from the beach, but at this point I was more than ready to get away for at least a little bit to go live the "college life," whatever that meant. Coming from a big, Irish Catholic family of five kids, where I fell second in line, the idea of some "freedom" was liberating! We had seven humans and two bathrooms, so someone was always knocking on the door. We often had a full house of friends sleeping over or stopping by. My older sister, Kerry, and I shared a room, plus having three younger siblings always just a few feet away, privacy was something I rarely experienced. Our house was the house everyone loved to come to, and the door was always open (literally).

I grew up in the most beautiful little beach town of Lavallette. We lived in a gray cape style house on the bayside, and the salty ocean was just up the street. Friday night was pizza night, Saturday morning we had chores before heading out for the day, and Sunday morning we went to church, followed by bagels and crumb cake.

We ate ice cream out of coffee mugs and often had our hair set in soft rollers (which never felt soft to sleep in) the night before a special occasion or holiday. It was predictable and safe and filled with love, even amidst the chaos. If you happened to stay at our house over a weekend, you had a blast, but you also did chores and went to church with the rest of us.

My mom loved a full house, and more kids were always the merrier for her. My mother was a kind, loving, patient mother of five, and an adored elementary school teacher for over 25 years. Mommy loved her students and always went the extra mile for them because she felt that they deserved it. She went so far as to give out our home phone number in case they forgot something or had a bad night . . . and they called, many times.

Joan Auer was born on June 13, 1947, in the Bronx, New York to my loving grandparents, Mary (Naughton) and Edward Auer. My mom was also one of five siblings and had dreamed of having a big family of her own one day. She had two older brothers, Richard and Edward, an older sister, Katherine, and a younger brother, Martin. She attended Preston High School and went on to Fordham University, where she graduated cum laude. She later received a double master's degree, summa cum laude, in Education and Reading, from Georgian Court College.

Joanie began her career teaching Kindergarten at a Catholic school in the Bronx. In the summers, she would rent a beach house with her girlfriends at the Jersey Shore. In the summer of 1968, my mom lived with 6 girlfriends, one of whom was Gail Fitzpatrick, a friend of a friend, who would grow to become my mom's best friend. In September of 1971, Mommy and Gail moved out of their family homes and rented their first apartment together on the Upper East Side, in New York City.

My mom was so many things, including a huge sports fanatic. If her beloved Bronx Bombers (AKA the Yankees) or New York Giants were on TV, she was shouting like she was at the actual game.

I often joke that we were born with pinstripes! But nothing was as intense as a New York Knicks game. I am certain that this love of hers had something to do with the John Starks (the Knicks star shooting guard) poster that hung over my bed for years. Eventually, John Starks was replaced with a Grateful Dead bears poster, which more accurately depicted my style in my late teens.

My mom had a warmth about her that was evident to everyone she encountered. She had a way of making people not only feel seen but valued and loved. It was a gift she fiercely possessed without even trying. No one could give a hug quite like she could, so strong and yet genuinely comforting.

Enter Fort Coleman (Colie) Brice Jr., a clamdigger from Lavallette, a true "local" through and through. Colie was born to his namesake Fort Coleman Brice, Sr. and his mother Doris (Hance) Brice. He had older twin sisters, Collette and Dorrie, and a younger brother, Robert, aka Ribby. Colie graduated from Point Pleasant High School and later went on to attend Ocean County College. He served in the United States Navy as a swim instructor stateside during Vietnam. He was a talented carpenter by trade, taking great satisfaction in his craft. Colie also was a proud volunteer fireman for over 50 years. He loved taking a boat ride down the bay, clamming, fishing or just cruising, and he loved Schaeffer beer. My dad also had two young children, twins, Colie and Collette, from his first marriage when he met my mom.

My dad was a simple guy, and for the most part, went along with whatever was asked of him. All my favorite memories with my dad revolve being in or around the water. After a hard day of kindergarten, my dad would pick me up to go fish off the beach. He would let the air out of the tires on his old Suburban and let me sit on his lap to "drive" on the sand. He would tell me about "Charlie the seagull" and teach me how to cast the rod. He was the definition of "salty" to me, and the older I have gotten the more my appreciation grows, to be so lucky to have grown up at the Jersey Shore.

Meaghan and Dad October 23, 1986 in front of our infamous big blue van

Joanie and Colie met at a bar at the Jersey Shore in the summer of 1971 when their love story began. Joanie was renting a beach house with her girlfriends. When the summer ended, Colie would make weekend visits to Manhattan to visit Joanie. Pictures of my parents from their early days together show two young, twenty somethings who were very much in love.

Colie and Joanie, Lavallette 1972

Joanie and Colie dated for two years and married in June of 1973. In September of that year, my mom began teaching at Hooper Avenue Elementary in the Toms River Regional School district. It took some time to adjust to year-round living at the beach, as my mom was very homesick for her parents and siblings. Within just a few years, her sister Katherine, and her family, her brother Edward, and his family, and her parents all moved to the Jersey Shore. In addition, during this time, her best friend Gail and her husband, "Big Ed" (Praslick) moved to Middletown, New Jersey and would come down the shore nearly every weekend to visit with my parents.

In February of 1977, Joanie and Colie welcomed their daughter, Kerry, into the world, and my mom began her greatest role. Having her support system around when she brought Kerry home made the transition into motherhood that much sweeter.

The worst day of my mom's life came on December 13, 1978, when her sister Katherine died suddenly at age 40, leaving behind her husband and her two daughters, Denise, age 11, and Jean Marie, age 7. As a child, Katherine had suffered from Rheumatic fever, in fact she was a poster child for this debilitating disease. In her mid 20's she had to undergo an open-heart surgery. The surgery was successful and enabled her to live a very fulfilling life as a mother, wife, sister and friend. But on that dreadful day in December, just days after her 40th birthday, while working at Macy's, Katherine had a massive heart attack and died instantly. Her sudden death left a massive hole in the hearts of the entire family, and the shock was impossible to absorb.

Even though Katherine was many years older than Joan, they had a very special, close-knit relationship. My mother never missed an opportunity to tell us about our "Aunt Sissy", or to remind us how lucky we were to have each other as siblings. For years I would carry a wallet size wedding picture of her because I just liked to look at her. She was gorgeous, and the picture made me feel a closer connection to the woman I had heard so much about, who died before I was born.

Aunt Gail, my mom's best friend, told me that the years after my aunt's death were devastatingly painful for my mom. She shared that mom returned to teaching and her master's program, but after that she just wanted to be in bed. My dad would call Gail during the work week to make sure that she and Big Ed planned to head down for the weekend, so she could spend time with my mom, while Dad and Uncle Big Ed would spend time with Kerry, who was just a toddler at the time. Aunt Gail said that when Mommy told her that she was pregnant with me, it felt like a sign that she was finally beginning to emerge from the depth of her grief. I did not get to personally witness my mother's early grief, but I could feel just how deep the pain was in her words and actions throughout the years.

On April 22, 1981, I, Meaghan Auer Brice, was born. Unfortunately, I was not the brother that Kerry had hoped for, but I did give my mom another reason to keep pushing through her pain. Three years later, in March of 1984, my parents welcomed another baby girl, Gail Katherine, (GK for short), and our sisterhood expanded.

But grief unexpectedly knocked at my mom's door again in March of 1985 when my grandpa, Edward Auer, peacefully died in his sleep and reunited with his daughter in Heaven. I wish I could remember more about the humble, kind, and loving man everyone talks about, but I was not quite 4 years old when he died. My memories are limited to being in the back seat of his big sedan and getting a lollipop at the bank drive-thru.

I found it unbelievable that my grandfather was drafted in March of 1944, at the age of 37! He was forced to leave his beloved wife, Mary, with three young children at home. While serving in the Army, he fought in Europe and in The Battle of the Bulge. He was a decorated veteran, awarded two Purple Hearts, two Bronze Stars and Battle Ribbons. My mom's brother, Uncle Eddie, is a vault of stories from his father's heroic past and I am always eager to hear them. Although my memories are vague, I have always been proud to be his granddaughter. He was a true American hero.

After her father's death, my mom stepped into a more active role with her mother. My grandma had never learned to drive, relying on my grandpa for most things, so she would tag along with us in our big blue van on outings from the mall to the soccer field to the grocery store. My grandma held her own grief close to her chest, longing for her beloved and living with the unbearable loss of her daughter. She had experienced significant pain in her lifetime, managing through WWII with young children, praying my grandpa would return alive and living in challenging conditions for many years.

Grandma was a tough, Irish cookie and she loved her family fiercely. As kids, we loved visiting her at her house in the quaint town of Island Heights. She always had cold cuts and Little Debbie snacks for us, and depending on the time of day could be found enjoying her "daytime soaps" or Wheel of Fortune.

Uncle Eddie and his wife, Aunt Gerry, lived down the street from Grandma, so they helped with her care too, and together they took the next steps. My cousins, Mary Jane, Jennifer and Jeffrey were also frequent visitors to Grandma's house while they were still in high school, and then throughout their college years and beyond whenever they came home to visit.

On April 16, 1986, Joanie and Colie welcomed Brendan Edward (a boy!) and on October 1, 1988, they welcomed Brian Thomas (another boy!). We were now complete. Five kids, two working parents, a golden retriever named Kelly, and a frog that outlived his life expectancy. (R.I.P. Lucky). In later years, we added a chocolate lab named Murphy, and a cockapoo, Bailey, named after my mom's favorite movie character of all time, the one and only, Mr. George Bailey from *It's a Wonderful Life*. And it truly was.

Over the years, with the demands of long days at school, work, and extra activities, those carefree days my parents once knew would lead to many nights falling asleep on the couch, or in the recliner, before rallying the troops to bed. I noticed my mother's grief would interrupt moments throughout the years, whether she became tearful or just sad at random or unexpected times. But she always modeled the importance of honoring the memories of her sister and father. Their absence in her life was noticeable and yet she talked about them so much that it made us feel like we really knew them and that they were a part of our lives still. On Christmas Day and Easter, before heading to Aunt Gerry and Uncle Eddie's house, we would make a stop at the cemetery. We prayed for my aunt and my grandpa, standing around my mom, witnessing the pain through her tears. Then she would collect herself and we would go on to celebrate the day. I never could have imagined that I'd reenact these moments with my own children years later in the same cemetery.

When I was in my freshman year of high school, my grandmother's health really began to decline. It started with her memory. She became convinced that I was stealing from her, and it was heartbreaking to repeat the defensive conversation, "Grandma, I would never take your money." Over time, my mom and Uncle Eddie would make the challenging decision to move Grandma into an assisted living facility. My mom struggled with this, but knew that she needed that higher level of care, and as a full-time working mother of five, she simply could not do it herself. Although Grandma resisted going initially, she did okay for a little while. She seemed to enjoy the social aspects, and was making friends and getting involved, despite being so forgetful.

Once Grandma was out of her house, we had to prepare it to be sold, which required an enormous effort. Traveling down memory lane appeared to be filled with both joy and sorrow for my mom. I recall clearing out a drawer in the nightstand and finding beautiful wartime love letters that my grandparents had exchanged and shared them with my mom. They were written with such raw, yet beautiful emotions, with the pain and loneliness of missing each other so deeply pouring out of each one. I treasured that discovery, as I could feel their profound love for each other through their words. The process of packing up and cleaning out the house clearly took a lot out of my mom, who at the time was still running five kids all over the place and teaching full time.

Unfortunately, Grandma's health continued to decline and eventually she had to be moved into the nursing home section of the facility. I hated it there, mostly because my grandma was wilting away and could barely take water off a sponge the size of a Q-tip. I never had a relationship with my paternal grandparents like I had with my mom's mom. Watching Grandma die was the first heartache from grief that I experienced. And witnessing my mom watch her mother die was just as agonizing. I was 15 and had no idea that the next level of grief would bulldoze this one and it would only be 3 short years later.

I was fortunate to grow up in a loving household, but it was often chaotic, so when it was time to go to college, I was ready to spread my wings! My first semester was a real dose of freedom. I had fun, a lot of fun, maybe too much fun. Thanks to kegs and eggs, pregame parties, late night parties, pizza and bagels, I had no trouble at all gaining the "Freshman 15" and then some and I was having a great time. But when I look back at my time at Scranton, before everything changed, what I remember the most are the beautiful budding friendships, laughing so hard I could pee my pants, impromptu dance parties, bonding with strangers who were becoming family, and walking to mass on Sunday nights after a weekend of drinking and dancing and being young and free. It was awesome.

On a random Wednesday in January of 2000, while home on my freshman winter break, I begged my parents' permission to go back to school for the night with my childhood friend, Colleen. Colleen also went to Scranton, and we lived across the hall from each other. We wanted to see our friends who had returned for winter sessions.

I would be returning to school in less than two weeks, but after experiencing the "freedom" of college, I was itching to get back. I was pleading my case, but the weather was supposed to get bad. My dad had the Weather Channel playing as background noise in our house 24/7 and the reports of a major winter storm heading our way was heard loud and clear, and so my parents did not want me to go. However, I persisted until I eventually got my way. Yup, I was a brat. Forcing that trip is a major regret and my night was hardly worth the worry that I put my parents through. I called home when we got there to let them know we arrived safely, and exchanged "I love you's", never imagining that it would be the last time.

The next morning, I called home to check in. My dad answered and said that my mom and my sister, Kerry, had been in a car accident, but everyone was okay. For nearly the next two decades, almost every call he would make, or message he would leave, would start with "Hi Meags, it's Dad, everything's okay." But everything was *not* okay. He said that my mom was just getting checked out in the local hospital and that Kerry was heading to Jersey Shore hospital because she injured her leg. I only sort of believed him. I realized later that he said everything was okay because he just needed to get me home safely. As soon as I hung up the phone, Colleen and I got in the car and drove back home in terrible icy, snowy conditions. The storm had come as predicted.

Colleen experienced the worst day of her life on Christmas Eve while in the 5th grade. Her sister, Laura, who had just turned 21, was driving home from work on the Garden State Parkway and was in a fatal crash. Colleen idolized Laura; she was much older, so cool, and beautiful. She was an amazing artist and a diehard Troy Aikman fan. Her family's collective heartbreak during that time was tremendous. Laura had been taken to the same hospital that Kerry was taken to because it was for more serious trauma, and that frightened both of us. We analyzed the brief conversation I had with my dad repeatedly. Something just felt off and we could not get home fast enough. When we finally pulled up to my house, there were tons of cars out front. My heart was racing, and I could hardly breathe. Oh my God, *Kerry* was all I could think. Everything was NOT OKAY. Something was VERY wrong.

As I approached the house, my cousin Jeff walked outside to greet me and said three words I will never forget . . .

"Your mother's gone."

I screamed. I cried. I tried to wrestle myself away from the well-intended embraces of my family members as they came outside to console me. I became numb. I felt like I died, like I wanted to die, and I'm pretty certain a part of me definitely did. When I finally went inside the house, I found my three younger siblings, Gail Katherine, Brendan and Brian, sitting on the stairs waiting for me. They were lined up one by one like we would do on Christmas morning. Except they weren't waiting for Santa, they were waiting for me because our dad was at the hospital with Kerry, and our mom had just died. I will never forget their faces that morning, they all looked so frightened, devastated and lost, desperately seeking solace in my eyes, which I could not provide. I felt an immediate shift in my pain and my heart broke again, this time for them. I was 18, but they were so young: 15, 13 and 11.

Earlier that morning, while taking Kerry to work, my mother's car skidded on black ice and crashed. She hit her head and had a brain aneurysm, and in a second, she was gone. My mom never even had a chance to make it to the hospital. THIS WAS NOT FAIR! I wasn't sure how we would move beyond that day, beyond that moment.

Later that day, I went to the hospital to see Kerry, who had been badly injured in the accident. Earlier that morning she had held our dead mother in her lap. She too, was numb. Our life felt like one of those tragic movies that I would never want to watch.

In the evening, we had friends and family gathered in the kitchen, talking and crying, everyone in shock. Amidst the commotion, I remember hearing someone open the front door, and my best friend, Emily walked in. Emily had been at school in Philadelphia and took the longest bus ride through terrible wintry conditions to get to me.

Emily's worst day of her life took place in October of 4th grade. She came home from school and discovered her dad had suffered a massive heart attack and died after playing tennis earlier that day. He loved playing tennis, and he also loved sailing. He was a great friend to many, and, from all the stories I have heard, an incredible husband and father.

Emily was introduced to me the summer before 5th grade through our mothers, a few months after her dad died. I never had the pleasure of meeting him, but I felt like I grew to know him through Emily and her siblings over the years. Emily was going to be in my mom's 5th grade class that fall, and our moms thought we should meet. They were right. She became like a sister to me, and we were inseparable almost immediately. She never spoke much about her grief, but I knew it weighed on her heart. Emily loved the chaos of my house and would stay with us every moment she could. My mom adored Emily and treated her as her own. When Emily walked into the kitchen that night, I hugged her so hard, and we cried together. I was beyond grateful she made it home because we needed each other so badly at that moment.

I could not sleep at all that first night. I was sharing my sister's twin bed with Emily, sobbing, thankful that she was next to me. At some point, I wandered into our family room and saw my dad and GK. My dad was staring out the window toward the bay and the night sky. I stood next to him and stared too. Then I began to squint, like I couldn't believe what I was seeing, but he saw it too. The shape of a cross appeared in the sky, in the form of a glowing bright light. Daddy said, through his cracked voice and tears,

"Mommy's okay, she's trying to let us know." I'm still not sure exactly what it was, but it was such a comfort to us in that moment, staring into that dark, cold January sky.

In the coming days our aunts, uncles, cousins and close family friends would help us plan and prepare for a funeral. Family and friends were in and out of our house like a revolving door. My dad's long-time friend, Tim Ryan, owned a funeral parlor and he helped take care of many of the funeral arrangements. Another friend, John Perillo, dropped off a Suburban from his car dealership. After the accident, our family car was totaled, and we did not have a vehicle big enough to fit all of us. Expected and unexpected people showed up for our family, like small blessings, left and right.

My cousins took my siblings and I shopping, and we walked like zombies through the mall to find nice outfits to wear for the services, praying we wouldn't see anyone we knew. I hated everything I tried on since I had gained so much weight my first semester, but I just needed to buy something black that fit. I hated being in public. We prayed and we cried, and we cried some more. At night I would lie awake, fearful of sleep, unable to close my eyes.

My siblings and I decided to write letters to our mother to put in her coffin. Kerry dictated a letter over the phone from the hospital that our cousin Katie typed for her. I had so much to say. I was so sorry for making such a fuss about needing to get away for the night. I wanted her to know how much I loved her and how much I appreciated everything she did for me.

Despite having five kids, my mom made us each feel so special and so loved. She made a fuss about everything. The older I got the more I pushed for my independence, and I know now, having teenagers of my own, this had to hurt. Somehow, I just assumed she would always be there. Whenever I was excited or anxious or dealing with a heartache, she was there.

I had been particularly heartbroken from a breakup with my high school boyfriend on my 18th birthday. If only I had known, it would be the last birthday I would get to spend with her. In an effort to cheer me up, she planned a special evening to have all my girlfriends over to celebrate. It was such a perfect night with decorations and ice cream cake and munchies and lots of laughs. She always went above and beyond, not just for her children, but for everyone who was lucky enough to know her. She was truly the most selfless person I have ever known.

I recall frantically making a list of "Things Mommy Would Say" right after she died so I wouldn't forget anything. I was suddenly flooded with panic, fearful that I would not remember her or the things she told us. I felt if I made a list while it was still so fresh, then I could not forget her. To this day, I still do almost everything on that list and have passed several of these "Mom-isms" along to my kids as well.

REMEMBER MOMMY ALWAYS SAID.....

Bow your head when you say Jesus
Bless yourself when you pass a church
Say a prayer when you see an ambulance
Stand up straight
Curl your hair
Put on some make-up
SMILE
Call me!
Go to church
Don't be mean to anyone
Do the laundry
Don't put everything in the dryer
Keep the house clean
Say Hail Mary's
Visit the cemetery every holiday
Iron your clothes
Help your brothers and sisters
Walk the dogs
Dry the bathroom floor
PRAY
Save your dolls
The secret to clazone's
Help around the house
Always say I love you when you leave
A kiss and a hug to everyone

Kerry had to be transported by ambulance in a wheelchair with a nurse back-and-forth to the viewing and funeral, then back to the hospital. She sat in the front row observing the hell that was now our life. It was surreal. I will never forget seeing my mother in the casket. I will never forget kissing her head or how cold she felt. I touched her hair and rubbed her head. I literally fell to my knees because standing was impossible. It was a pain I had never quite felt before, it was hard to breathe, it is also a moment I will never forget.

Once we had a few brief moments alone with her, we braced for the line that we were told was already wrapped around the building on a brutally cold and icy January day. We closed the casket to the public because we felt it would be too painful to see her in this way, especially for the many current and former students who would come to pay their respects.

I stood with my dad by the casket as we comforted the mourning faces in front of us. The line at the funeral parlor felt endless, flooded with family, friends, and students. Every once in a while, I would glance back at the casket, knowing that her body lay inside. Everyone loved her, everyone mourned her, but she was *our* mommy. It felt so unfair, she was so good to so many. Why did she have to be taken? It was the most beautiful and heartbreaking tribute, and I felt like I was having an out-of-body experience. One minute I was in tears and the next I recall leaning over to my dad and saying, "Why are these people so sad? Don't they know Mommy is in Heaven?" And he replied, "I think they see the five of you without a mother and feel sad." I was so dissociated, which was probably a blessing so I could get through that day. When the line finally ended, I took off my heels and walked around the funeral parlor barefoot, reading the cards on the flowers that filled the room. I was still in shock. When would this nightmare end so I could wake up?

The next few weeks were a painful blur. My dad had put a public thank you statement out to our local radio station as the outpouring of love and support from our community truly was felt and appreciated. He then dedicated Elton John's beloved classic, *Candle in the Wind*. The chorus still echoes in my mind,

"And it seems to me you lived your life
Like a candle in the wind
Never knowing who to cling to
When the rain set in
And I would've liked to know you
But I was just a kid
Your candle burned out long before
Your legend ever did"

Shortly after, I was encouraged and lovingly "forced" to return to Scranton. I wanted to stay home. I wanted to help Kerry, who had a long road to recovery, and it broke my heart to leave GK, Brendan and Brian. Everything about it felt wrong, but my dad felt that it was best for me and what my mom, a strong believer in our education, would have wanted, so reluctantly, I went.

The immediate support we received in the weeks following the funeral was overwhelming. All the women who knew and loved our mom coordinated a food train and helped to prep the kids for the school weeks ahead. We really needed all the help we could get in the beginning. My mom had done everything, and we were lost.

My friend's parents were very generous too, purchasing me a laptop so I could go back-and-forth between school and home on weekends and keep up with my schoolwork. Another friend's mom gave me money for books and other incidentals I might need when

I returned. I was overwhelmed by their generosity. For a few years, at Christmas time, I was given a generous envelope of cash from an anonymous donor to be used for presents for the kids. To this day, I do not know who it was from, but it was so greatly appreciated and well spent making Christmas morning just a little brighter. In time, the extra helping hands slowed down. Eventually people had to go back to their own lives and had their own families to take care of. We understood and were truly so grateful for their help in our time of need when we didn't even know what we needed.

Shortly after returning to school, my resident advisor, Marcia, asked me to come down to her room. She was crying and said that she didn't want to leave what was in her hands at my door. Marcia handed me a box of chocolate roses and a Valentine note that my mom had filled out on parent's weekend back in the fall. I looked down and saw my mom's beautiful cursive handwriting and the endearing sentiment, "To my middle sweetheart" that she would always affectionately write on cards and notes to me. My heart cracked open again and the dam burst. *Oh Mommy*, this hurt too much.

The three-hour drive home from Scranton became my normal Friday routine. I did not have a car at school my freshman year, so I would take a ride from anyone headed to New Jersey for the weekend. While I wanted everyone at home to need me, the truth was that I needed to be home with my family. The grief was so intense, and while my friends at school tried so hard to be supportive, I was broken. I came home on weekends to help with laundry, track and baseball practices, and school projects. When I was home, I felt that I was exactly where I needed (and wanted) to be.

One weekend, a few months after my mom had died, I scheduled myself a much-needed hair appointment as a little pick me up and I was really looking forward to it. I was a little teary eyed as I walked in to see our hairdresser Bev, who had been doing all of our hair, including my mom's, for many years. I smiled as I caught her eye and when she looked up and saw me, she had a very confused look on her face. "Hi honey, your appointment was last Saturday. I left a message at the house for you, but I never heard back." My stomach dropped and the tears started streaming down my face and within a few seconds I could not catch my breath. I was having my first panic attack. Bev quickly walked over to hug me and guided me to a chair. She brought me some water and talked me through it. She reminded me to breathe, and she told me that if I could wait for a few minutes, she would squeeze me in when she wrapped up with her current client. I just nodded and whispered a thank you. I was embarrassed and felt so fragile. I knew this was about so much more than missing my appointment. I am type A by nature, so forgetting my appointment was unusual. But I had been running myself into the ground trying to get through my college courses during the week and then commuting home every weekend for a quick 48 hours. This was not the "college life" I had envisioned. It was unsustainable, and my grief felt like a tidal wave had washed over me that day. Something had to give.

By December 2000 I packed up my room at Scranton and finally was allowed to come home for good. I'm pretty sure everyone was happy, but no one was as happy as me! In January, I enrolled myself at Ocean County College, my local community college. It was a transitional semester for me and was just what I needed to find my way to Georgian Court, a local university I could commute to the following semester, the same school my mother received her master's degree from while she was pregnant with me.

Those years felt like a blur. I helped raise my siblings along with my dad and Kerry. I stayed up late to make Easter baskets and stuff Christmas stockings. I wanted my younger siblings to have what I had, even though I knew it would never be the same for us again.

Somehow, despite the endless chaos our family created, I was finally starting to get back on track. I found a balance between school, helping at home, doing my internship at Ocean Hut Surf Shop and waitressing at The Bayside Café. My coworkers at Bayside, Patti, Bunny, and Ellen, were, and are still, like family to me. My boss, Tom, consoled me while working on the first 4th of July after my mom died. You never know how or when certain events will trigger grief, but when they do, it's nearly impossible to stop it. Tony and Mary Beth, the owners of the surf shop, offered me the utmost love and support. Those coworkers, those friends, held me up through an impossible time and allowed me to laugh through tears. I also began dating the man who would eventually become my husband, and my heart was starting to fill with a love I had never known before. Life was not perfect, and there was still a tremendous loss felt in our home, but we were slowly healing tiny pieces of ourselves. We always talked about Mommy, and we still do, and somehow that helped us then and I think it still does today.

On January 20, 2025, while writing and rewriting this book, we marked the 25th anniversary since my mother's death. I had so many emotions emerge that I felt the need to write and express how I was feeling in that moment, as it has proven to be a cathartic release for me time and time again. Here is what I wrote and then posted to my socials . . .

> 25 years and one day ago was the last time I knew a much simpler version of myself . . . the me . . . before my mom died. I was only 18.
>
> This anniversary hits different and hurts more than I could have imagined, mostly because I am so sad for me and I am sad for you, Mommy, that you didn't get to experience our lives and the lives of your adult children and incredible grandchildren.

There is a very clear before + after for me. I didn't know she would be forever gone. We had no time to prepare, and for that I am grateful. I also didn't know who I was about to become, but in the past 25 years, I have become a version of myself that I am really proud of, a version of myself that holds others in a way I didn't know possible. I didn't know how the trajectory of my life would change that day or the parts of me that would struggle with the what ifs, the could'ves or should'ves, even after all these years. I have come to realize that it doesn't really matter though because I am truly living by those most true parts of me . . . I am authentically shaped through my heartache.

I am proud of who I have become . . . Heartbroken, grief stricken, overly sensitive, easily triggered, frustrated, jealous, grateful, blessed, pained, joyful, silly, enthusiastic, compassionate and so much more.

I will never know why 25 years ago had to be the last day, but I will always know that I eventually chose getting better over being bitter. I chose seeing the good instead of always feeling like woe is me. Even still I have felt the unfairness of our tragedy many times. But I know that in my heart, she has never really been gone. My unwavering faith has sustained me. My mother has not only been the most influential woman in my life, she has continued to be a guiding light as a mother, a grandmother, a friend, a comfort, and truly my angel from above.

25 years later is the year that I hope to bring to light the book I poured my heart and soul into for the last two years. I will forever be grateful for the love and support of our family and friends and those that continue to share memories of our beautiful mother . . . you have no idea what that means to all of us.

And for my husband and my children . . . you see me in my most vulnerable and raw emotions, even then, I know she's always with us. I can't live without her being a part of our story. There is no way we would be who we are today without her unconditional love and guidance. Thank you for embracing a spirit of a woman you've never met with such love and tenderness.

Mommy, I will never ever stop remembering you, talking about you, and doing my best to emulate the parts of you that have made me feel who I am today . . . the most proud daughter ever to be. I would not ever trade my short 18 years with you for anyone else. You are my light. I love you and miss you forever and always. Xoxoxo

CHAPTER TWO

the loves of my life

Erin and I met in high school, and we just clicked instantly. Erin was a brown-eyed beauty with a great olive complexion. We shared a mutual love of the beach and The Cranberries, the beloved Irish rock band. She was soft-spoken and so easy to be around. She was the baby of her family and possessed a very chill, relaxed vibe, which was a good balance to my often loud and outgoing self.

Erin's worst day of her life happened almost exactly a year before mine, on January 18, 1999. Her brother, Doug, was on break from college, commercial fishing to earn some extra money. Doug loved being in or around the ocean, so it was a great job for him. Between being in the hands of mother nature and the dangerous, unexpected conditions that local fishermen encounter, Doug's boat was lost at sea. Devastatingly, his body was never recovered. There was a lack of closure after such a horrific tragedy, and the pain was unimaginable.

Despite my best efforts, I did not really know how to support Erin in her grief. But one year later, I joined the unpopular Grief Society. It's amazing how young people can come together in such dark times. When you've gone through it yourself, you fall into step, supporting the next person who's unwillingly joined the club. We leaned on each other and supported one another. For two college girls experiencing immense grief, having someone who was going through it at the same time was its own kind of therapy. We understood the healing power of our friendship, and we appreciated not having to put on a front with each other. If we were having a bad day, we were just there for each other. We often called and emailed, and when she would come home from school, we spent a lot of time together.

In early 2001, while hanging out at Erin's house, her dad presented us with a gift. I remember him saying something like, "*You girls have been through so much in the last two years. I have a lot of domestic airline miles to spend. Since you have the same spring break this year, we think you should go somewhere. It just must be within the United States.*" For the first time in a long time, I was really excited for something. Erin and I, without hesitation, knew we wanted to go as far away as possible. Beach, sun, cute surfer boys . . . San Diego, here we come! I reached out to my childhood friend, Erik, who had been living in Pacific Beach with a few other guys from back home. He said Erin and I were welcome to crash at his place. He had other people staying that week too, but we would make it work. Honestly, a couch or a comfy pillow on the floor in San Diego felt like a royal destination for us at that time. We gave him our flight info, and a few weeks later he picked us up at the airport. I had no idea what this trip would mean for the direction of my life.

Our trip started with an authentic Mexican burrito from Adalbertos and the immediate realization that everyone in San Diego was beautiful. We were so happy and grateful to have gotten away from home, away from our pain, even if just for a few days. When we arrived at the house, we saw many familiar faces from high school.

I'm not sure exactly how it started, but I remember feeling an almost instant connection with Jay when we saw each other. We had gone to the same high school, but he was two years older, and we never really talked before, although I definitely knew who he was. Growing up at the beach, I always had a soft spot for surfer boys and Jay fit the mold to a tee. He was super cute, cool and laid back, quite the opposite from me, usually talking a mile a minute, which my mom always referred to as "my gift of gab."

Jay lived with Erik in San Diego until that previous December and had just moved back home to New Jersey, down the street from me. He was also visiting for spring break to squeeze in another week of surfing. I had really never believed in coincidences, but I am a true hopeless romantic, and it was hard not to get ahead of myself and start planning our happily ever. I couldn't quite explain it yet, but I knew that whatever was happening between us was something special.

The week flew by, and Jay and I were both feeling a strong attraction to each other. Erin and I would spend the days together, grabbing breakfast or lunch at a local spot and then walking down to the beach to people-watch and sunbathe. We were thriving in our element and so grateful to be out of our constant grief for a few days.

In the evenings, we would catch up with the guys for dinner, drinks and hanging out. One night we were walking home from a party at a neighbor's house, and I remember Jay reaching out to hold my hand. My heart was giddy and yet so comfortable. At the end of the week, we celebrated Jay's 22nd birthday with a great dinner and some cocktails alongside Erik, Erin and all the other friends who were in tow that week. It was a fun night! Early the following morning, Jay flew home. When I arrived home the next day, I had a message from him checking in and making sure that I had a safe flight home. Insert heart stop and squeals!

Later that week, we had our first real date. Jay invited me over to his house for dinner. He made us corn flake crusted chicken, and it was delicious! I was so used to eating a bowl of cereal for dinner, so this was a real upgrade. I loved that he took the time to prepare something, and he clearly took pride in it. I knew that this was just the beginning, but my feelings were so strong from the start.

The ease of being together and getting to know each other came so naturally. We both enjoyed life in and around the water, we loved riding bikes, meeting friends for a night out, watching Jeopardy on the couch, and going to bed early (we still do).

My life was too intense to have something casual. If you were a part of my life, you were a part of my family. Jay, an only child, embraced Kerry, Gail Katherine, Brendan and Brian and they squeezed him right back. He fit in perfectly with us and I counted my blessings. To be honest, it is hard not to like him. He has an easy-going disposition, he is extremely loyal, hardworking and considerate, and my siblings could all see this from the beginning too. I loved being in love, but I hadn't realized how much I needed someone to care for me. I was 19 when we started dating, going to college, waitressing, helping raise teenage boys and managing a household. I was often on autopilot, until Jay slowed me down.

As I was putting the finishing touches on the Easter baskets that year, I saw headlights in the driveway. Easter morning was just a few hours away and I wanted to make sure that it was special when GK, Brendan and Brian woke up. I knew that they probably no longer believed, but that didn't stop me. My mom created pure magic for us all until she died. It didn't matter if we believed or not, because the Easter Bunny and Santa *always* came to our house. When the car turned off, I could see it was Jay walking to the front door with tulips (my favorite) in his hands. It was such an unexpected and sweet surprise. When I pointed to the flowers and asked, "What are these for?" He smiled and looked over at the Easter baskets filled with chocolate bunnies and little goodies. "You are always taking care of everyone else; I wanted to take care of you tonight."

In the years that followed, we grew stronger as a couple. I wanted forever to start yesterday, while Jay was more patient. We had fun, we traveled, we worked hard, and we were falling deeply in love. Jay was attending Stockon College to become a teacher and I was in the Business program at Georgian Court. He would come visit me at the Bayside Cafe on his mornings off for coffee and a "bomber" (pork roll and cheese with home fries on the side) and I would go visit him bartending after my night classes for a much-needed Long Island Iced Tea. In the early days we traveled to Rincon, Puerto Rico and the Outer Banks in North Carolina. We often traveled with our friends and would return with tan lines and some incredible memories. But my siblings always remained a priority throughout, celebrating their many milestones along the way of confirmations, graduations, birthdays, holidays, and the day-to-day tasks like homework, PTA meetings, practices, and meets.

A few years after Jay and I started dating, my dad was falling in love again, too. My dad had known Liz for many years, having been a friend of her husband before he passed from brain cancer. She had also been my Brownie leader when I was in kindergarten. One day after church, both sitting alone in their pews, my dad asked Liz if she wanted to take a boat ride, and she said yes. Through combined heart ache and grief, they built a beautiful relationship together, and their love story began.

During this time, my family would have more ups and downs, which led Jay and I to have some ups and downs too, but we always pulled through. One of the prominent downs was when my dad was diagnosed with squamous cell carcinoma, throat cancer. Dr. Google basically told us that he would be dead in months. After having lost Mommy only a few years prior, we couldn't handle this. *He never smoked. How could he have throat cancer?* My mind spiraled to the worst case scenario and it was too much to bear. How would we live without him? Why would this be happening to us? The unfairness of the diagnosis loomed in the air as we were still very much coping with life without Mommy.

I remember shortly after the diagnosis we were driving in the car together and my dad said, "You'll have to teach the others how to drive stick shift, ok?" In our family, we prided ourselves on driving a manual transmission. "No way, you will do that, Dad." I could feel the lump in my throat and swallowed hard so I wouldn't lose it. We didn't know if he would make it, but we had to keep the faith.

Thankfully, the incredible team at Memorial Sloan Kettering Cancer Center in New York City saw things differently than Google. It would not be easy, but it was treatable. Daddy would have surgery that required an incision from ear-to-ear across his throat. He joked that he would look like Frankenstein. But the surgery was far from funny. If you've never been inside a cancer hospital, the fear and dread is palpable. The doctors would come out, and if they had bad news, then they would pull you into a private area where the sobbing was heard through the partitioned office walls.

But Daddy's surgery was a success! Thank God! He needed chemo and radiation to finish the job, as the cancer had invaded his lymph nodes. This particular time period is a bit blurry, but I do remember that he got very thin, and his face looked jaundiced for a while. His saliva was barely present, and he had cases of Ensure stacked up all over the house because it was the only thing that he could keep down. The one thing that stood out most was his optimism. After the initial shock of hearing the devastating words, "You have cancer," he rallied. Dad knew how powerful his thoughts could be. He survived; we survived. And after his recovery, he would be the first one to reach out to someone with a new diagnosis and tell them how important it was to stay positive. I was so proud of him.

Loving me and my family was complicated. It was never "easy" or "normal". But when we were all together, we were infectious. We laughed through our tears, and dark humor became our sturdy companion. Hard times would always bring us closer, and we felt stronger leaning on each other. Yet, I often found myself feeling guilty, torn between wanting to spend time with Jay after school and work, and being available and present for my siblings.

I vividly remember a dream I had around this time where I was driving home and speeding because I was worried that I would get home too late for Brendan and Brian. When I walked into our house, I saw my mom, dressed in white pants, a white sweater and holding a white, patent leather purse. She was a bright, glowing vision. My mom seemed like she was in a rush to leave, almost like she was trying to leave before I got there. I said, "Mommy, oh my God, how are you here?" and she replied, "I never leave my babies alone." When I woke up, I sobbed, feeling like I had just really seen her. Although I was comforted by her message that she was always with us, it also made me miss her more than ever.

I knew that I put too much pressure on Jay sometimes. My grief was heavy, and I was not a typical 20-something. My priorities and responsibilities did not resemble those of my peers. I needed to unload some of my pain and stress, and Jay allowed it. We were young and in love, and somehow, we navigated through and around the grief and pain that would surface in me. The anniversary of my mom's death and Mother's Day were always, and still are, extra difficult. But I didn't hide my pain from him, I simply couldn't, and he would have seen right through it anyway. He also continued to help me through challenging times with "the kids". I would float back-and-forth between home and Jay's house. He made me feel happy and safe, and I knew that he truly loved me. I knew I had found my person.

When the words, "Will you marry me?" came out of his mouth on April 21, 2006, I think I said yes. I honestly can't remember saying anything. It was a chilly evening and the sky was gray. I had suspected for months that a proposal was coming but I did not know when. After getting home from work that evening, Jay asked if I wanted to go for a boat ride and that's when I became suspicious. It was not exactly ideal conditions for a cruise, but I said yes without hesitation. We jumped on the boat and headed out. When we approached the middle of the bay, Jay put the boat in neutral and said he thought something might not be operating properly. He told me to stand by the bow of the boat and when I walked around, he followed me and dropped to one knee. My heart was screaming with joy. I had impatiently waited for this day for over 5 years, and that moment was worth every second of waiting. It was just us on an old, crappy, little boat in the middle of the bay, wearing hoodies and drinking cold beers. It sounds like a country song, and it was perfect. The next chapter of our lives was beginning, and I was floating on cloud nine. When we got home, we popped champagne and called family and friends, inviting them over to celebrate with us. It was a magical evening!

I couldn't have prepared myself for the intense grief that would interrupt my joy during our engagement, but I was determined to not allow the grief to ruin it for me. I felt strongly that my mom had a hand in our relationship, somehow, someway. I knew that she would have loved everything about Jay, especially that he was a teacher, and more importantly, a Yankees fan. Even still, I had some moments that were tough. My Godmother, Aunt Gail, took me wedding dress shopping and although my mom's absence was felt, we still had a beautiful day, and the gown Aunt Gail bought for me made me feel like a princess on my wedding day. Jay and I planned a beautiful wedding, working together as a team on every detail from choosing the venue, taste testing for the menu, requesting the songs that the DJ would play, and deciding on the seating arrangements.

As I was in the shower getting ready for our rehearsal dinner, Jay knocked on the door to check if I was okay. I had been in the bathroom for a long time. I did not have cold feet, I just missed Mommy so much and couldn't believe that she would not be with me on my wedding day. I was crying so hard that I had to be on my knees to steady myself. I couldn't stop bawling my eyes out and my breathing was heavy. Jay gently told me that the rehearsal was starting soon, but that I should take my time. Slowly, I got myself out of the shower and got ready and we headed to the church for the rehearsal.

After the church, we headed to our rehearsal dinner. For our rehearsal dinner, our friends, Jimmy and Christine, captured the essence of us and hosted the most perfect evening at their restaurant, Surf Taco. It had a simple, yet romantic feel, with votive candles and fresh flowers on the tables, cold beers in a steel tub, the delicious aroma of fresh Mexican cuisine and the sound of Jack Johnson playing through the sound system. It was such a fun night surrounded by our closest family and friends, and it was exactly what we needed.

That night, I slept at home one last time with my sister, Gail Katherine. It was bittersweet. I was ready to begin my married life with Jay, but I still had some guilt and sadness moving out for good and leaving the kids. GK has such a big heart. She's so much like our mom in that way. She was excited for me and cheered me on, and if she was feeling sad that this chapter was ending for us, she didn't show it.

On the morning of May 11, 2007, I woke up smiling ear-to-ear. The tears were gone, and I was ready to marry my best friend. My mom was with me that day, I could feel her presence. I desperately wished she was there with me physically for every moment, but I embraced her spirit and allowed it to offer me some comfort. I spent the morning getting ready at Aunt Gail and Uncle Big Ed's house, sipping champagne and savoring the special time with my bridal party, and then with my dad and brothers when they came by to take pictures.

Brendan, Me, Daddy and Brian

We arrived at the church in a beautiful white trolly, and I could not have felt more joy and love in my heart. Seeing Jay at the end of the aisle, waiting for me to say "I do" was so special. It was a "pinch me" moment. Our church was packed with family and friends, as well as current and former students of Mr. Hughes, all so happy to be sharing in our special day. After the church ceremony concluded, the bridal party all jumped in the trolly and popped more champagne and cracked open cold beers and headed to our reception. Our wedding day was spectacular, and we threw a damn good party, if I do say so myself! Everyone danced the night away. It was truly a celebration!

We waited until the summer to go on our honeymoon to Hawaii since Jay was a teacher. As a surfer he had longed to experience surfing in Hawaii, and we were so excited to take in this beautiful island together for the first time. We had two incredible weeks in Maui and Kaui. We enjoyed delicious coffee in the morning, walking through town, and sipping on cold beers in the evenings. We chatted about what it would be like to live here, pointed out the school he could work at and just enjoyed the fantasy of living in Hawaii. We explored various local beach spots, hiked trails that led to beautiful waterfalls, went fishing on a charter boat, saw some giant sea turtles up close and personal, got dressed up for a fancy dinner one night and ordered room service the next night. We loved the energy and people of Maui and the town of Lahaina where we stayed, it was breathtaking. Kaui was so lush and green, and we soaked in the beauty all around us.

On our return home we were both quite anxious and excited because we would soon be picking up our Yellow Labrador puppy. He was eight weeks old. During our honeymoon we decided on the name Kai for our pup, which in Hawaiian means “Sea”. Kai was the runt of the litter and immediately stole our hearts the moment we laid eyes on him. Our friends and family loved doting over him too. We were now a perfect little family enjoying this sweet stage of our life.

After solely doting on Kai for nearly two years, we knew we were ready to expand our family. Our hearts grew more than we could have ever imagined on April 21, 2009, when we welcomed our son, Shane Edward, into the world.

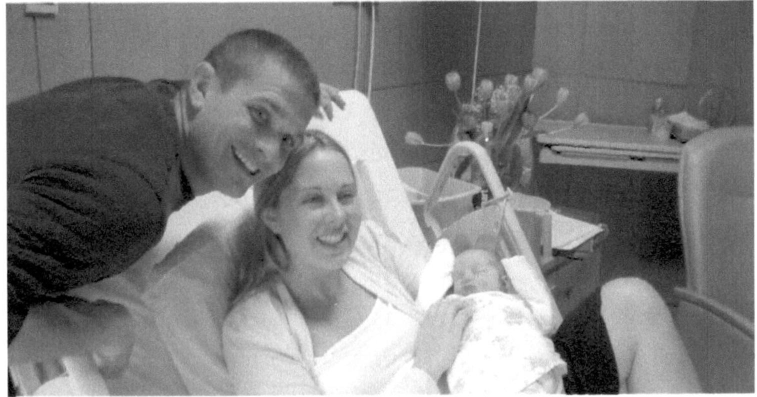

Two years later, on May 20, 2011, Emily Joan made her debut and joined our crew. Jay and I were overjoyed, and overwhelmed, becoming parents and adjusting to this new world. Of course, Shane, and Kai, were very protective, big brothers from the beginning.

The pain of my mom's absence was felt throughout my pregnancies, from not being able to share the first ultrasound picture, to her not being at my baby shower. I had so many questions about my changing body during my pregnancies and about what to expect, and I wondered if she had similar experiences. Mostly, I just longed to have my mom be a part of this next chapter. At times the ache was debilitating. But what surprised me the most was the healing that I began to experience when I became a mother. I was once again experiencing a mother/child relationship, only now *I* was the mother. The gift of motherhood is the greatest blessing I could have ever imagined.

Watching Jay as a father has surpassed any expectations I could have dreamed of. He is so hands on, is a total Mr. Fix it (thank you YouTube videos!), and has proudly worn the "Coach" title for over a decade for various baseball and soccer teams, for both Shane and Emily.

As a family, we love, we support, we feel deeply, we encourage, we fight, we make up. We are far from perfect. We make mistakes, but when we do, we talk, we apologize, and we seek to better understand each other. I learned this early on from my mom. My mom had the best way of moving past an argument, she modeled apologizing and the ability to restart the day, at any time of day. When she was ready, she would always say, "Good morning, Meag" and I would reply, sometimes reluctantly, because it felt silly, "Good morning, Mommy." That simple exchange gave us all the ability to reset, and we used it often. Jay and I live, and lead, by example, and most importantly, we model actions that are aligned with our values. The four of us make a really great team and I could not be prouder of our little family.

Our little family of 4, long before they were teenagers

Our “not so little” family of 4, Summer 2024

CHAPTER THREE

the worst day of my life—part 2

(3)

Shane Hughes 11-3-17
Writing Personification

The worst day in the world

"It was a sunny beautiful day," I said. It looked like the best day ever. Brids sang there songs and the wind blew softly. As I opened my toy chest, I was like a kid with 8,000 chocolate bars.

As I was playing it started to get brighter. I got into comfy clothes. My dad came to check on me. My dinosaurs all good to play with. I ate my breakfast and brushed my teeth. I heard my mom scream "NO!" I thought she was watching a show so it didn't bother me. I was wrong. I went down stairs and asked "What was going on?" I sat next him and repeted myself "What is going on?" I looked outside it started pouring rain.

My dad said "you don't want to know." I realy wanted to know I thought.

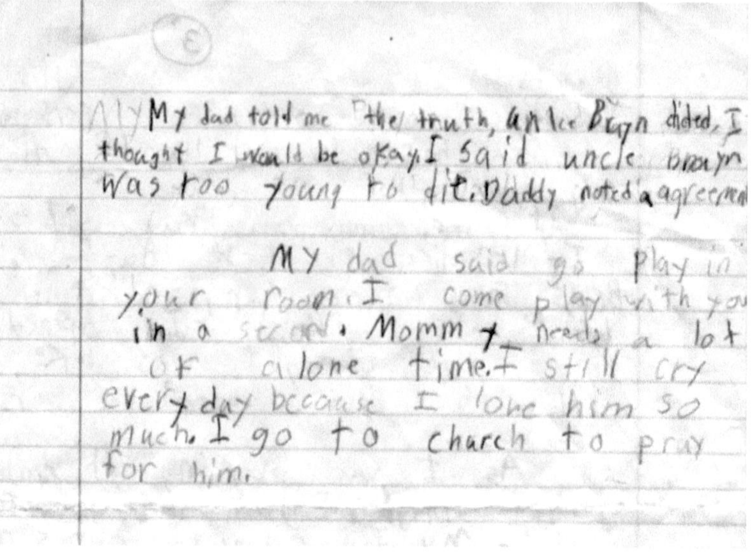

My dad told me the truth, uncle Brayn dided. I thought I would be okay. I said uncle Brayn was too young to die. Daddy noted a agreement

My dad said go play in your room. I come play with you in a second. Mommy needs a lot of alone time. I still cry every day because I love him so much. I go to church to pray for him.

The Worst Day in the World by Shane Hughes 11-3-17

"It was a sunny, beautiful day," I said. It looked like the best day ever. Birds sang their songs and the wind blew softly. As I opened my toy chest, I was like a kid with 8,000 chocolate bars.

As I was playing it started to get brighter. I got into comfy clothes. My Dad came to check on me. My dinos are all good to play with. I ate my breakfast and brushed my teeth. I heard my Mom scream, "NO!" I thought she was watching a show so it didn't bother me. I was wrong. I went downstairs and asked, "what was going on?" I sat next to him and repeated myself, "what is going on?" I looked outside and it started pouring rain.

My Dad said, "you don't want to know." I really wanted to know I thought. My Dad told me the truth, "Uncle Brayn died." I thought I would be okay. I said Uncle Brayn was too young to die. Daddy noted in agreement.

My Dad said go play in your room. I come play with you in a second. Mommy needs a lot of alone time. I still cry everyday because I love him so much. I go to church to pray for him.

The unimaginable happened, and that was how Shane recalled it in 3rd grade, a little more than 3 years after Brian died. It never rained that day, and my heart aches that he has this horrid memory. My sweet boy, who loved his silly Uncle Brian. Uncle Brian died by suicide on August 15, 2014, a few weeks before Shane started kindergarten.

This is how I remember it . . .

It was a sunny Friday morning in August. We were all home, Jay and I enjoying coffee in our pj's, the kids and Kai playing and giggling, and we looked forward to enjoying the beautiful summer day. But a little after 7:00am I heard my phone ringing and saw *Daddy* on my screen.

"Good morning, Dad. What's up?"
"Hi Meags, are you home? Where is Jay?"
My heart stopped beating. He didn't say "Everything is ok."
"Yes, we are both home. WHAT is going on?"
"It's Brian." His voice was trembling.

I don't remember exactly what he said after that. I couldn't breathe, I couldn't bear to feel what was erupting inside of me. I recall screaming for my husband and running upstairs to get away from my children so they would not witness my self-destruction. I was unsuccessful. They saw me, they heard me, and I know I must have scared them.

Jay yelled, "What is going on?!" I could only moan back, "Brian died. He killed himself." As the words left my lips, I could see Jay crumble too. It was disbelief, it was denial, it was how the fuck did this happen? Before I hung up with my dad, he told me to call my sisters and tell them because he was with Brian. He was also with my other brother, Brendan, and his fiancé, Amy. Amy had found him first.

I attempted to call my brothers-in-law first, in the hopes that they could tell my sisters, or at the very least, be there with them. My sisters both answered when they saw my name pop up on their phones. Those were the worst phone calls I have ever had to make.

Brian was the baby of five. He was the only one with dark hair and big brown eyes, and although he was smaller in size, his personality and energy could light up a stadium. He was smart, quick-witted, silly, and handsome. After our mom died, my role in Brian's life became a mix of sister and mother. I was now going to PTA meetings, doing his laundry, trying to stay on top of schoolwork, monitoring what he was doing online, and helping to get him where he needed to be. I also tried to be "cool", but I worried about him a lot.

Brian had his share of reckless behavior throughout the years. Since he is not here to defend himself, I will not go into too much detail, but it was not insignificant. During Brian's high school and college years he maintained his good looks, quick wit, and big personality. Let's just say that Brian knew how to have a good time and that often left us worried and frustrated. He often pushed it just a little bit too far. After he died, I began to think of his actions with more sadness. Had he been so reckless because he didn't care if he died? In retrospect, was his behavior a cry for help? Or was he just trying to have a good time? We will never know for sure. When you lose someone to suicide, the questions, the "What ifs", haunt you for a LONG time, possibly *forever*.

The summer of 2014, Brian was very busy, or at least this was the impression he gave us. His band was playing a lot of gigs, and his bartending schedule was full. Whenever Jay and I could, we would catch his band play. I loved bragging to people at the bar that the singer was my brother. No one asked me, but I told them anyway. I was really proud of him.

Because Brian's schedule involved a lot of late nights, which led to sleeping during the day, and I was a working mom with a 3-year-old and 5-year-old at the time, our lives didn't overlap much. I also felt like he blew me off a few times that summer because he had other things going on. Maybe he was avoiding us, maybe not. Again, I'll never know for sure. But he also expressed his love for us, and he would randomly reach out or stop by. He posted this to Instagram on April 10, 2014.

One of the last times I remember seeing Brian was on Mother's Day. I was at church with Jay, Shane and Emily. When it was time to exchange the sign of peace, I turned around and saw Brian in the back. Brian didn't come to church very often unless we asked him to come for something specific. I didn't expect to see him. My heart sank. My Mother's Days were always bittersweet, grateful for my children, while desperately wishing my mom was there with us. But for Brian, it was just bitter.

He missed her in a different way. The rest of us were married with children, or soon to be married, and had partners to lean on, but even though Brian had had a few long-term relationships with some great girls, he had not yet found "the one". He was only 25, but I think that may have fueled his loneliness, which he was good at hiding from us. If only he knew how much we all still ached for her, maybe we could have worked more on healing as a family.

Brian and Mommy used to snuggle on the couch every night. He truly was Mommy's baby, but in an instant, she was gone forever. I don't think his heart was ever going to heal from that pain. I believe that his greatest love was our mom, and in some way, I imagine his emotional maturity was fractured because of her sudden death. How could anyone match that kind of love, or even come close?

A few days before the services, I once again found myself wandering around a store for something to wear, this time with my sister Kerry. What I really wanted to do was put a bag over my head. After finding nothing, we agreed to wear something we had and that we would not wear black. Brian deserved some color!

We used my house as a home base for planning the services and gathering as a family, to eat, to drink, to cry. It was Grand Central Station for a week. My girlfriends, Michelle and Lauren, and my in-laws, seamlessly took Shane and Emily over the next few days as we focused on making Brian's sendoff something beautiful. It was such a dark time for our family, it did not feel appropriate to have Shane and Emily around witnessing everyone's erratic emotions. My dear friend, Erin Ryan, whose family owned the local funeral home, helped us create a day Brian deserved. Erin's process made each moment and decision manageable, from deciding on the casket he would lie in, to picking up the clothes he would wear. I'll never forget her tender care during that time.

Brian's friends were also a huge part of his life. They too ached, and many struggled with their own "What if's" and "How the fuck did we not see this happening?" Like I said, Brian was good at hiding it. Even though his closest friends saw more of his dark side, they could not have prevented what happened. They showed our family love and support in ways we did not know we needed, and in return we loved and supported them back as we tried to comfort each other. Brian was just 25. Our baby brother, a son, a nephew, an uncle, a Godfather, a cousin, a friend.

The night before Brian ended his life, we spoke on the phone around 11:00pm. I was at a party at a friend's house and wanted to see if he was coming. "Even Daddy's here, you should come!" I remember saying. He said that he wasn't going to make it and asked if I was going out afterwards. I laughed and said, "I don't think so, it's already way past my bedtime." He didn't say that he was having a bad night. He didn't ask me to stop by on my way home. But I would have gone. I would have stayed all night, and when the morning came, maybe I would have saved his life. But he never asked, and I didn't know how desperately he needed someone. He never wanted to worry or burden us. The next morning, as the sun was rising on a beautiful summer day, Brian, Mommy's baby, died by suicide.

Grieving after Brian's death was different. I was not 18 this time and wasn't only worrying about my siblings, even though I *was* very worried about them. I was married now with two small children, and I was broken and in the dark. Brian was Emily's godfather, but she was still so young, she would only remember him through stories and pictures. I was so mad *for* her. Shane knew and loved his Uncle Brian, and that was its own kind of hard, and I ached witnessing his confused grief. In the months and years following his death, Shane and Emily continued to ask questions about Brian's life and death. And just like my mom always talked about her sister, I have done the same, sharing stories of childhood memories and giving them full permission to express their own anger and sadness around his death.

People would say things, trying to be helpful after Brian's death, but death by suicide makes people feel uncomfortable. I did not have the energy to manage the comments about Hell or Purgatory. I knew his soul was in Heaven with Mommy. I knew that he would not be punished for all eternity for his broken heart. My God is loving and forgiving, and I chose to believe that because the alternative was torturous. Yet blame and shame continued to swirl all around us.

I hated closing my eyes for a long time. I would let the shampoo get in my eyes in the shower and sting just so I didn't have to shut them. I didn't want to see the images I created in my head. I didn't want to see what I imagined Brian looked like on that sunny morning, but I couldn't avoid it. At nighttime, I would dread the dark. I needed a light on to sleep, and even then, it was brutal. In the beginning, when it was still warm outside, I remember waiting until the crack of dawn to sneak quietly outside and lay on a lounge chair with Kai, my sweet boy, and try to sleep for a little bit before everyone else woke up. Somehow, if the sun was up, I could rest easier. It was less scary to me than the darkness of night.

My husband carried me through those days. One night I woke up to Shane in our bedroom and I started yelling at him, "Brian! Brian!" He didn't know what was going on, and I'm sure that I scared him. After going through the old photos for the services, I saw such a similarity between Shane and Brian at that age. It was really messing with my head.

A little more than a month after Brian died, we rallied like never before. If there was a rally in our bones, it was September 19, 2014. My brother Brendan was marrying his high school sweetheart, Amy. Brian was supposed to be the Best Man. Growing up, Brendan and Brian were always lumped together, whether they were playing or fighting, building forts, or seining in the bay. It was hard to have one without the other. They both loved our Mommy and they both suffered immensely when she died. We always said, "Thank God for Amy because she really saved Brendan," and we meant it. Sister-in-law does not seem close enough to how I feel about Amy, she *is* my sister. Amy continued to love Brendan through his grief. And now it was compounded because it was her grief too.

We vowed to make the day of their wedding a true celebration. We had the rest of our lives to be sad, so that day was about them. It was both heartbreaking and beautiful. While my sisters and I danced to Marvin Gaye and Tammi Terrell's *"Ain't No Mountain High Enough* " for our sister/brother/mother/son dance, a video montage played in the background with pictures of our family. I couldn't watch it, I just remember dancing and singing and embracing the moment, which Brendan deserved. It was sad enough that we were dancing with him because our mother was deceased, but the raw nature and newness of Brian's death loomed all around us and it was a lot. After that dance I headed to the farthest bathroom I could find to allow myself a hearty, private cry. I walked in and saw my sister Kerry. I guess we had the same idea. Once we regrouped, we reentered the celebration and put the tears back on hold.

Left to right: Me, Gail Katherine, Brendan & Kerry

Weeks and months would go by, and I cried a lot. I remember many times sinking down in front of the dishwasher sobbing, trying to hide myself from the kids while they ate dinner on the other side of the kitchen island. They knew I cried, and I tried my best to stay strong for them, but the pain was oozing out of me, and I could not contain it.

I distinctly remember one night that fall, the sky was clear, and the stars were bright, and we were on our boat returning home from Monkey Point, the home of one of Brian's best friends. His parents were a huge support for Jay and me in our grief. I believe that our relationship was mutually healing. That night, many of Brian's friends came by Monkey Point to skate the half pipe and to see us. Shane, Emily, and Kai loved it there and they loved being loved by Uncle Brian's friends. The sunset was a magnificent backdrop to our silhouettes. The night sky was so healing, but as we slowly cruised home, it hit me HARD. The kids had fallen asleep in the cabin and music was playing. I went to the stern of the boat, and I screamed in agony. I was angry and aching, letting out the kind of guttural cries that cause physical pain.

Returning to work was hard. Returning to Mom Life was hard. Returning to friendships was hard. *Everything felt hard.* It felt hard for a *really long time.* Then, one day, I couldn't tell you when or why, I could shower with my eyes closed and eventually I could sleep without a light on.

As I write this chapter, I am on my lunch break parked by the Manasquan Inlet. The sun is shining, seagulls are dipping and singing, and the fishing boats are heading in and out. It's a serene sight. It is August 15, 2023. Today is also 9 years since Brian died by suicide. Today is hard, *really hard.* My tears are flowing once again. I don't need an anniversary to be reminded of the pain of Brian's death, but days like this just hit differently. Grief is far from predictable, especially when it hits unexpectedly. But on anniversaries, there always seems to be a cruel memory loop playing on repeat in my mind all day long.

While writing this book, my friend Christene Martin and I were discussing our anniversaries, too many to count for both of us at this point. Christene's first worst day of her life was when her dad died while we were in 7th grade. He was a loving father, husband, and a beloved priest in the Greek church, and his 30th death anniversary had just passed. She said, "It's pretty wild how each stage of life brings different feelings from a reality that is so old. It's like the only constant for the last 30 years is that he has been gone, but we get to re-experience that loss when new things happen in our lives." She expressed it so beautifully that I wanted to share it here. Also, I couldn't agree more. What a strange and complex understanding, that sadly, you can really only know, if you know.

Brian Thomas Brice, my smiling baby brother

CHAPTER FOUR

how could we do this again?

"Your father is unresponsive. What do you want us to do?"
"WHAT?!"
"Your father suffered a heart attack, he is not responding and it has been some time."
"SAVE HIM!"

Earlier that morning, before the sun came up, I picked up my girlfriends, Beth and Erin, and drove to Newark Airport to fly to New Orleans. Beth and Erin had become friends of mine through our children's CCD program, where we were all volunteer teachers. Leading up to the trip, we all felt way out of our comfort zones, and anxious about leaving our families for a few days, but we were doing it!

Although I had a full-time job, I was looking for ways to make more money, and selling skincare from my phone became a convenient option. Our "side hustle", Rodan and Fields, was having a convention and I was drawn to the headliners, Mel Robbins and Rachel Hollis. I had listened to their books, *The 5 Second Rule*, by

Mel and *Girl, Wash Your Face*, by Rachel, and followed them both on social media. This side hustle helped open my mind to the possibility of MORE. I still couldn't put my finger on what "more" actually was for me, but I believed in myself and my ability to dream a little bigger and stretch beyond my comfort zone. One thing that I knew I desperately wanted was more control of my time, as I think most working humans do, especially when they have young children.

As we were sipping our Starbucks and waiting at the airport gate, my phone rang with a local number I didn't recognize. I usually wouldn't even answer such a call, but because it was so early, I did. And that's when I heard the doctor shouting on the other end.

Let's rewind a bit. Two weeks prior to my New Orleans trip, in early September of 2018, my dad had gone to the hospital. He had blood in his stool and his doctor recommended that he go to the hospital to get checked. He asked Liz, his longtime love, not to tell us right away. Dad was always worried about scaring us and he did not think this was a big deal at the time. To his point, my siblings and I had become very easy to scare and automatically assumed the worst.

This was not my dad's first rodeo, although he appeared healthy on the outside, he was not the epitome of health on the inside. Before the cancer diagnosis in the early 2000's, he had a stent put in during a cardiac catheterization, which led to a pretty serious staph infection. After the cancer diagnosis, he had more medical issues, including a stroke, which he miraculously recovered from.

Brendan and I stayed in the ER with him after the stroke into the wee hours of the morning while he waited for a room and a bed. He could not articulate words or coordinate his movements. He was so frustrated, and we struggled to keep him calm. We were so scared what this would mean for his quality of life. It was the longest night, and our minds were racing from one bad thought to the next. Finally, a room opened, and once he was settled, we went home to get a few hours of sleep. When we returned the next morning, he was awake and talking and making jokes. Brendan and I were stunned, and sleep deprived, wondering what had happened in those few hours.

During one of his earlier medical episodes, Dad told me about a dream he had where he thought he was dying. He said that he was moving towards a light and my mom appeared and stopped him, telling him that it was not his time yet and that the kids still needed him, then she turned him around and sent him back. He strongly felt that message, and I can vividly remember tears rolling down his face as he recounted the dream.

My dad had nine lives, or so it seemed. His tolerance for pain was unmatched and he rarely complained. His famous quote whenever anyone asked him how he was feeling was always, "Good shape for the shape I'm in." Whenever I would ask if he needed anything, he'd only ever request "Just some cherries and cherry juice please," and this was usually when his gout would flare up.

But this time would be different. At the hospital he was told that he would need a colonoscopy to get a better view of what was going on. Following the colonoscopy, he was in a great deal of discomfort, and for a guy with high pain tolerance, this was alarming. Liz called us at that point and said that my dad had been complaining that something was bothering him. When they checked him again, the doctor could see that they had perforated his colon during the procedure. They would need to go back in and remove a piece of his colon, after which he'd need to stay in the hospital for about 10 days. Dad was not happy about this. The discomfort following the removal was very painful and he hated being in the hospital that long. I called him to check in on my way to work, the day before I was leaving for New Orleans. He had been there about 10 days at that point and was scheduled to be released the next morning. He first had to be cleared by several doctors from the cardiologist to the gastroenterologist, and it appeared that everyone was giving him the green light. But even though he was to be released within 24 hours, he sounded down. There was no trace of the reassuring nature that I was used to. I told him that I loved him and that I would be over to see him as soon as I got home.

After yelling, "SAVE HIM!", the doctor abruptly hung up on me. I stared at my phone in a panic, then called Liz. I had no idea what the severity of my dad's condition was, and I could not think straight. She told me that she was on her way to the hospital and would call me when she got there. I looked at Beth and Erin and they asked me what I needed, I said, "I need to go." In unison they both replied, "Then go."

Thankfully, I had driven us to the airport, so I had my car there. But getting out of a large international airport and to the shuttle bus to the parking spot was like speed walking through Mars. The world around me was upside down and spinning backwards. All I could think was, *Get to the car. Get to the* car. Once I navigated my way out of the parking lot and onto the road, I called Jay. Just as he was about to wish me a safe flight, I interrupted him and blurted out what was happening. He said that he would get the kids to school and asked that I reach out as soon as I knew what was going on. Then I called my siblings, or maybe Liz did. I was in such a panic that I could hardly focus. I knew that I would be the last to arrive because I was coming from Newark, which was over an hour away from the hospital. I just kept praying to God to watch over Daddy and relied on the GPS to direct every turn because I could hardly breathe, let alone pay attention to where I was going.

When I finally arrived, everyone was crying and gathered in the ICU waiting area. It was bad. "He is intubated, and he was unresponsive for a long time. He's not awake," Kerry told me as she held my hand, walking me into his room. Seeing my dad in that state was paralyzing. Only the sound of the ventilator could be heard over the pounding in my chest. "*Oh, Daddy*," I cried. The doctors explained that after rounds that morning he went into cardiac arrest. By the time they stabilized him, he had already lost a lot of oxygen and there didn't appear to be much brain activity.

Over the next five days, we allowed the doctors to try everything possible. Day two was my dad's 73rd birthday. For the first time in decades, he would not be taking his annual birthday dip in the Atlantic Ocean. I kept replaying our conversation from a few months earlier, "Meags, if you can save me, save me, but if I'm ever a vegetable, don't." He had had so many big health scares over the years, and at this point my mom had been gone for over 18 years, so we all knew that it was not only important, but also necessary to communicate things like this.

The night my dad received his last rites, it was just Liz and I. Father Michael, our pastor, spoke to Daddy and we prayed together. We couldn't even look at each other. We both rubbed his arm, held his hand, cried, and prayed. My heart broke for Liz, watching her experience this heartache of losing the love of her life for the second time. Our families had blended beautifully. We felt at ease talking about her late husband and my mom. We truly love Liz and witnessed the joy and companionship she brought to our dad's life. And Liz's daughters and sons-in-law loved my dad right back. Our mutual losses had made our connection solid. As kids, (albeit adult kids) we were happy to see our parents happy, and our kids became cousins to each other, celebrating Thanksgiving and Christmas together. We were a big, blended family, and we knew how fortunate we were. Their love story lasted for over 15 years, but it was supposed to last a lot longer. They were supposed to grow old together. This wasn't fair. But still, we prayed, and we hoped.

September 17, 2018, the morning of day five, the doctor called me just as I was parking in the hospital's garage. She was warm and patient and reminded me that we would have to make a decision about my dad's end-of-life care that day. They had done everything possible, but nothing had worked. I told her that we had made our decision, but needed to wait until our close family members could be present that afternoon. As I walked inside, I called Jay to let him know. He had been back-and-forth to the hospital, was juggling the kids, and he had just begun a job as a principal in a new school only a few weeks earlier. He had his first Back to School night that evening, so I knew that he wouldn't be able to come back to the hospital.

Once we were all present, I took rosary beads out of my purse that someone had given me after Brian died, and I wrapped them carefully in Daddy's hands. The nurses asked us to step out for a moment so they could remove the ventilator. They were incredible. I don't know how they do what they do every day, but their compassion and patience was extremely comforting. A moment later, we all surrounded him again, rubbing his hands and his head. We prayed, we cried, and we told him that it was okay to go, that we would be okay. We told him that Brian was waiting for him. We said all the things we thought he needed to hear, if he could even hear us at all. Eventually, surrounded by his family, my dad took his last breath, and in that moment we all lost yet another piece of our hearts.

This felt very unfair. Hadn't we gone through enough pain? This was not his time, and we still needed him. We told him to go, but we didn't really mean it. We were now parentless adults who had also lost a brother. Our chaotic, happy family of seven was now down to four. *What the fuck?* I was pissed and I was sad. Those five days had wrecked us. It had been emotionally and physically depleting.

In a somber exit, we left the hospital and agreed to meet back at my dad's house as soon as possible. I picked up the kids and stopped home to grab the trays of food that had been delivered and a few bottles of wine. My kids had seen me through rough times and this was no exception. They hugged me and my heart hurt even more. The feelings were still so raw. Shane and Emily are so blessed to have a loving Grandma, Papa John, and Grandpa on Jay's side, and I am very grateful they have them in their lives. They are the only grandchildren on that side, and they are truly adored and loved. And yet still, I found myself feeling sad and bitter at times because they were never able to even meet my mom. I longed for her to be a part of their day-to-day lives, and now their time with Pop Pop was cut short too. My emotions were running wild, and I was struggling to manage my feelings.

Dad still owned our childhood home, and it was exactly where we all needed to gather. It was serene that evening, standing on the deck, overlooking the bay while the sun gently lowered herself to sleep in the background. Eventually the moonlight began to reveal her beauty and cast a calming glow over the water; it was a beautiful blessing in that moment. As I soaked it in, I prayed for strength to get through the coming days.

View from the deck at Briceland

Before leaving the hospital that night, we requested an autopsy. It did not settle well with any of us that our dad was cleared and scheduled for discharge in the morning, but then had such an uncomfortable night. The records showed that his nurses had been attentive to him throughout night. It was documented that he had several calls to the nurse's station, yet he was not seen by a doctor until the next morning. I couldn't help wondering if he could have been saved had he been seen by a doctor sooner. What if his increased discomfort began during the day and not late in the evening? My mind bounced around multiple scenarios. The number of times I had to go back to that hospital to get the rest of Dad's complete medical records was ridiculous, and I felt nauseous every time I parked in that garage. Once the autopsy was in, we shared it, along with his medical records, with a lawyer, who was also a trusted family friend. She reviewed everything, then sent us to a more specialized lawyer in the field. We weren't looking for a pay day, we simply felt that if the doctor could have or should have done more, then by exposing his negligence we could help save someone else. We were desperate for answers that made sense of how this happened overnight in a hospital.

After a few months of review, it was determined that the case wasn't worth pursuing because of my dad's many pre-existing medical conditions. I did not have years of legal fighting in me. But I will never feel that it was his time. I guess that's why I avoided writing this chapter for so long. It's been five years since my dad died, and I still can't fully wrap my head around it. Those five days were the longest we ever had to say goodbye to someone we loved, yet it was never going to be long enough.

In the coming days we planned yet another beautiful tribute, and once again my friend and funeral director, Erin Ryan, stepped in to help. My dad had been a volunteer fireman for many decades, so we would have a fireman's funeral, and he would also get military recognition for his time spent in the Navy, but I needed to find his DD214 form. *Ok, no problem.* If you could imagine a literal needle in a haystack, that was what I was up against. My dad had papers *everywhere* in his office. I'm sure that this was an organized system in his own mind, but for his slightly OCD, neat freak daughter, I was lost. I became upset and angry because I knew that he would have saved this important document, but I was also still steeped in grief and wasn't thinking clearly. After many prayers to Saint Anthony (and cursing my dad out loud) I stumbled across a shoebox in the back of a drawer stuffed so tightly that I could hardly open it. I opened the box and there it was! I picked it up and discovered his will underneath. "*How could you put such important stuff in a shoebox?*" I muttered to myself, along with a few other choice phrases. The will revealed that I was assigned as his executrix. *Oh, okay. What the hell does that mean?*

The following week we had the most incredible service to honor our dad. Our friends and family huddled around us once again to share in our grief, including many firefighters to honor Dad's 50+ years of volunteer service. The fireman processed through the church, all dressed in uniform, and they lined the pews. Their presence felt immense, which was both a comfort, as well as a heartache. It was an honor to have so many of them show up for our dad that day, it truly is a brotherhood.

During the homily, Father Michael, shared some inspiring words: "These firemen answered a call on their hearts. They each have a purpose. They are volunteers, and yet they choose to put their own lives at risk for the call to help others." He went on to speak more about their honor and sacrifice, then he asked the congregation, "What is your purpose? What is your heart calling you to do?" *Well,* I thought, *I have been trying to figure that out for years and I am starting to lose hope in ever discovering it.* His message was powerful and stuck with me long after that day.

The Lavallette, Ocean Beach and Seaside Fire Departments helped us with the send-off. We transported the casket in the back of a 1930's vintage fire truck, the same fire truck that carried Brian's casket four years earlier. Brian was laid to eternal rest next to my mom and her sister, Katherine. My dad's wish was to be cremated and have his ashes scattered in Barnegat Bay. After the funeral, we followed the fire truck in a procession through my dad's beloved Lavallette, past the fire house and our home (affectionately known as "Briceland"). Neighbors and friends stood outside and waved, and it was beautiful. After the procession, the casket was returned to the funeral parlor and transferred to a hearse to be brought to cremation, and we all watched somberly as they drove away. Then, when the hearse was out of sight, without much thought, we all jumped on the back of the fire truck in our dresses, suits, and sunglasses that hid giant mascara smudges and swollen, red eyes. We rode through the town my dad loved so dearly, the town he was born and raised in. In the midst of our heartache, it was a pretty epic moment.

Once Dad's ashes were returned to us, my siblings, Liz and I decided that we would wait until the one-year anniversary to scatter them. The weather was starting to get cooler, and we were not exactly sure yet how we wanted to handle everything. We did not want to rush it. In the meantime, I did some research and found a biodegradable turtle that was meant to be filled with ashes and then would slowly dissolve. I liked this idea better than just throwing the ashes, God forbid the wind blew them back at us!

When the turtle arrived, I brought it to Liz's house and together we opened the ashes and filled it. I had never seen cremated ashes before, and I hope I never do again. I thought it would be a good idea to use seashells to scoop the ashes into the turtle to keep it as natural as possible. Slowly, through a flood of tears, we did it. I hated that day. It was not what I expected, and I couldn't believe that those ashes were once him. It felt surreal and I was still in shock and very numb over his death. The only comfort was having Liz by my side. Helping her through that moment somehow helped me too.

About a year after his death, many of us, including our closest family and my dad's friends, piled onto our boats and headed out towards Hankins Island on a beautiful September night. It was truly a "local summer", when the tourists were gone, but the lovely summer weather lingered, my dad's favorite month of the year. We had a few beers and shared a few words of thanks to everyone who joined us to say goodbye and send Dad to his final resting place. It was a truly peaceful evening on the bay, the air was salty, and the sky was lit up with a beautiful sunset. Eventually it was time, so we placed the turtle gently into the water, along with some beautiful leis that our friends from Monkey Point had put together. Dad, having been a swimmer in the Navy, had a field day with us because he did not just float and sink as the instructions indicated he would, instead he swam for a while (several minutes, in fact!) right to where he wanted to be. We laughed through our tears and shook our heads at this "you had to be there to believe it" moment. It was then that I began to feel a shred of peace. Dad was now peacefully at rest, and I knew where to find him.

My role as executrix of the will and estate took on a whole new life of its own. I was proud to act on my dad's behalf and carry out his wishes, and I wanted to continue to make him proud of me, even after his passing. It was also a really hard job, and I had to pull up my big girl pants several times to have challenging conversations, or to even just push through my waves of enormous grief when I was overwhelmed.

My dad owned a few apartment units in town that he requested be sold, as per the will, and so this was my first major undertaking as executrix. It was a giant headache, filled with unbearable memories. I did not have any love for those apartments, and none of my siblings did either, so the fact that he wanted them listed for sale after his death told us that he didn't want them for us anymore either. I remember as a little girl the many times my dad would be called away because something broke at one of the apartments or a renter needed something. He was "the guy" they called for everything, which took him away from us more. One of the apartments was also the last place Brian had lived.

I didn't even like driving past the apartments after Brian died, and now, 4 years later, I had to be there regularly. At first, I had to collect the rent, and eventually I had to tell the tenants that in a few months we would begin remodeling the units so we could sell them per my father's request. I was uncomfortable taking my dad's place as "that guy" and was on the receiving end of many angry sentiments, but I reminded myself that it was temporary and kept going. There was no alternative.

In addition to the main units being sold, our dad's garage, which was attached to the apartment complex, also was being sold. The amount of stuff he had saved in his garage was overwhelming, so it was all hands-on deck to get through the initial demo and dump days. My sisters and their husbands, along with Jay, Brendan, Amy and I, got to work. My younger sister, Gail Katherine, had three young girls at home, a two-year-old and six month old twins, and I know that not being able to help much left her feeling frustrated and uneasy. She always stepped in when she could, but she was really in the weeds, and we knew that. My mind was in a heavy fog during most of that time, but as we got closer to the finish line, I was proud of what we had accomplished. The units looked better than before, the garage was empty, and we were able to sell each one.

Together, Jay, Brendan, Amy, and I had become a team, becoming each other's rocks when we needed it. Once we finally sold off the apartments, we were able to focus on the house. The house that we grew up in, the house we all loved so much. My siblings all agreed that we would continue to manage the summer rentals that our dad had started the summer before he passed. The maintenance, upgrades, repairs, etc., push us to the brink every spring like clockwork. It takes an enormous emotional toll on us. But each year as the rental season begins, we get excited for our repeat renters to see the work we poured into the house over the winter months, and then every fall when the season wraps, we are even more excited for it to be over. We are grateful that we can share our home with others, but we are even more grateful when we get it back. Maintaining it and improving it is a labor of love. Shane and Emily have witnessed many tears and seen a lot of sweat poured into the house over the years because often they are right there with us getting dirty in the off season, or they are with me at a BBQ, or at the beach, or on the boat when I get a call that there is a problem at the house, because usually the problems happen in the middle of a summer weekend. They see all that it takes to maintain the house that they love, too. I know that my dad would be proud to see Shane helping Brendan with a project, or Emily helping Amy and me with the decorative final touches. In this way, I keep him alive for them. I'll say, "Go grab Pop Pop's tape measure." or "That's in Pop Pop's office." or "Pop Pop would be so proud of you guys." It is time consuming and frustrating, but it is also so rewarding. Like I said, my role of executrix took on a whole new life of its own, but I wouldn't trade it for anything to keep our home, and the memories it holds, alive.

In the years since my dad passed, I see him through a different lens. I never thought of my dad as a businessman, but after stepping into his shoes, I see the smart real estate decisions he made over the years. We really appreciate our little slice of Heaven, and hopefully it will remain in our family for generations to come. Thanks, Dad.

CHAPTER FIVE

unconditional love and a pillow for my tears

Along with many others during the pandemic, we jumped on the *it's a good time to get another puppy* train that was taking place. We had been going back-and-forth many times, debating if it was fair to do this to Kai. He was declining in his old age and had been the one and only star of the show for so many years. But one day, while taking our now regular, late afternoon Covid bike ride, an adorable black lab marched past us with his people. Shane and Emily had taken off ahead of us, and Jay and I were slowly cruising home. We felt it was time and agreed that bringing a puppy into our home would bring more love and joy. And because I was now home so much, we wanted to take advantage of that. Emily, the dog whisperer, had already been begging for another one. She'd remember a dog's name before she'd ever remember the human's name! And it just so happened that the breeder we contacted was going to have a litter ready for pick-up in June, just a few weeks away.

We are not the type of parents who typically surprise our kids with major things. I've always enjoyed the anticipation and planning of fun things, so we usually include the kids in our travel plans, big events, and purchases. We are a close-knit group of four, but this life event was different somehow, so we intentionally did not say a word to our kids about getting a puppy. The day we went to pick him up was a day I'll never forget. We took the long car ride with the kids, who were very curious about where we were going. When we arrived to the address, we drove down a long and winding driveway, and pulled up to the garage. The garage doors were open and there were two women standing behind a folding table. I got out of the car alone as Covid protocols only allowed one person to go inside. I spoke with the breeders, and after signing the paperwork and getting all the important documents, I finally laid eyes on him and my tears began to flow instantly. *Hello sweet boy, I'm your Mommy.* I scooped up the puppy and headed back to the car. Emily and Shane started freaking out. Even Jay was tearing up. It was such a beautiful moment for our family. This was our new baby, and we were already in love.

Jay and I introduced our new puppy as Triton, the King of the Sea. We had tossed around so many names prior to getting him and wanted one that would complement Kai, "the sea.". Shane also was a huge fan of Greek mythology at the time, so it was very fitting. During the car ride home, we talked about the importance of giving Kai some extra love so he didn't feel resentful of the new puppy. Thankfully, Kai and Triton's love for each other was sweet from the beginning. Kai taught Triton how to exist in our home, how to be chill, and how to love his family.

While there were many early mornings in those first few months, Triton was such a good pup, and he fit seamlessly into our family. He was able to experience Kai's last year of life, while Kai was able to experience Triton's first year of life. There is no doubt in my mind that getting Triton at the time we did was a blessing that extended our sweet boy's life. Triton gave him more energy and was a wonderful companion, especially when we all returned to school and work. Triton would always find the perfect way to snuggle with Kai.

Kai and Triton, May 2021

By June of 2021, we knew that Kai was getting worse. We hated to see our boy suffer, and there was nothing we wouldn't do to save him. Over the years we had removed lumps and bumps, and even his happy tail (due to a cancerous tumor) to make him more comfortable and prolong his life. He began to struggle with the stairs and then even walking became challenging. And as summer approached, we knew it was his time. We called our vet who had lovingly cared for him since he was eight weeks old, and he told us to enjoy our night with him and to bring Kai to see him the next morning. That last night was agony.

Before the kids came along, Kai slept with Jay and I, but once the kids got older, he found his spot in Emily's bed at night, and when no one was home during the day, he liked to sleep in Shane's bed. But over the past few months, it became increasingly difficult for Kai to get up the stairs, so Jay would pick up the 90-pound pup and carry him up a flight of stairs just so he could sleep in the room with us. But that night we decided that we didn't want to cause him any additional discomfort, so we all slept downstairs with him, touching his paws, petting him, hugging him and kissing him with tears soaking our pillows. When the morning came, it was nauseating to think about what we had to do. The kids said their last goodbyes and gave him all the hugs and love they could possibly muster up.

When Jay and I arrived at the vet's office, our vet immediately told me to stop crying. I was not his patient, Kai was, and he needed him to feel as safe and comfortable as he possibly could. My initial irritation with his command briskly shifted to appreciation. I wiped my tears as best I could and told Kai how much we loved him, what a good boy he was, and that everything was going to be okay. It felt like forever, and yet not nearly long enough in those final moments with him. When we got back home, we all cried. Everyone took the day off from school and work, and we grieved the loss of our sweet boy together. We took Triton for a walk, slowly maneuvering through our fog, and gave him some extra love and attention.

The early days after he passed were so difficult, as he truly was the heart and soul of our family. Kai was able to absorb all the negativity from the outside world that we brought in and create a safe calm in the middle of the chaos. He was the eye of the storm. He was like an energy healer, and he gave us so much love. Having Triton after Kai passed helped so much. We didn't know how much we needed him. The only thing that would've been worse after coming home that morning would have been to come home to a house without a dog inside.

Triton has since taken over that special role in our family. He loves us fiercely, wants to go anywhere we go, and is a great snuggler. He's friendly, happy, and lives up to his name as the "King of the Sea", loving the boat and the beach, and even getting super sandy. Falling in love with a dog is so easy, it's the heartbreak when they leave us that is so difficult, and I know we will all be missing Kai for our lifetimes.

PART II

look for the light

I said: What about my eyes?
He said: Keep them on the road.

I said: What about my passion?
He said: Keep it burning.

I said: What about my heart?
He said: Tell me what you hold inside it.

I said: Pain and sorrow.
He said: Stay with it. The wound is the place where the Light enters you.

—Rumi

Welcome to Part II!

You made it! Stand up, take a deep breath, breathing in through your nose, and let a loud exhale out through your mouth. Stretch, shake it out, and get a tall glass of water and maybe even a hot beverage. I hope you feel the energy shift as you move into Part II.

In this section, we will take a deep dive into my healing and growth through my grief journey. I will include mindful exercises at the end of each chapter as a prescriptive call to action. You can use the space provided and write in the book, or you can use a separate journal for your entries. I encourage you to not look at the prompts as homework assignments or another thing on your to-do list, but rather an intentional investment into your healing. Make the time to be still and reflect, while you allow your thoughts to unfold on the paper. Most importantly, be as honest and raw with your responses as possible so that you can make the most out of each exercise. Speak from your heart, free of judgement and self-doubt. You may find that some of the prompts feel too difficult right now, and that's okay, they may be too hard right now. Feel free to revisit them when you are able. It is impossible to rush through our grief, so sit with it and when it feels okay enough, give it a try.

Writing can be extremely therapeutic, and as a clinician I recommend journaling to my clients often. By allowing your thoughts to be transferred to paper, you are freeing up precious real estate in your mind. Also, when we write, our thoughts and ideas tend to flow more freely. Please keep in mind that these exercises are not a substitute for actual therapy, but they can be a supportive companion along the way.

My intention and hope for you is that as you allow my story to resonate, you also look within and tap into your internal knowing, believing that you too can do something more meaningful with your grief. I have found that we do not just *move on* from grief, but we must ***carry on***. In the coming chapters, I will reveal to you how I have carried on.

CHAPTER SIX

hope and healing from an unexpected light

A few months after Brian died, Jay and I were invited to our friend's house for dinner. With Jimmy and Christine, it's always laid back, fun, and we can just be ourselves and unwind. Over the course of 25 plus years of friendship, our families have developed a genuine closeness and mutual admiration for each other.

During dinner, while the guys were chatting about the next surf trip, Chris leaned over and said, "I can see how much you're hurting, you're just not yourself." I agreed with her and told her how everything felt like a struggle. I missed my brother and analyzed his suicide relentlessly, including my own role in his life and death. I was unfulfilled at work, and I felt like I was constantly dropping the ball at home. Even things that had always brought me joy felt more like a burden. And it wasn't for lack of trying, but I could only fake it so much. I was just going through the motions. It felt good to be honest, even if it felt dark. Chris got up from the table and came back a minute later with a book in hand. She shared that the author was someone who graduated from our high school and that she hoped its message would help. Over the many years after my mother's death, I had read books on grief, but nothing seemed to help. I thanked Chris and tried to enjoy my wine and the delicious meal she cooked, thinking that I'd add the book to the stack next to my bed, knowing that she meant well.

Months went by before I picked it up. On a particularly hard day, I opened the book entitled *Discovering the Medium Within* by Anysia Marcell Kiel. I figured that I had nothing to lose. A few hours later, I read the book cover to cover. This was *not* a book on grief. Goosebumps, tears, curiosity, and hope consumed me. This woman was not just an author, she was also a healing medium, and I felt compelled to see her as soon as possible.

From first grade through my senior year of college, I was taught about Catholicism through my education. But my mother is the one who instilled this faith in me from the very beginning. She taught me that faith can be your greatest tool, believing in something greater than yourself and knowing that we are never truly alone. My Catholic faith has always been my north star and my moral compass. It gives me direction, hope and deep connection. And I am still very involved with my faith to this day. I taught CCD for eight years, I am a Eucharistic minister, and I attend mass regularly.

My parish also means so much to me. This is the place where my parents renewed their wedding vows. This is the place where each of my siblings and I were baptized. This is the place where we held my mother, my brother, and my father's funeral. This is the place where my sisters and I got married. This is the place where Shane and Emily were baptized, made their First Holy Communions, and their Confirmations. When I sit in the same pews that I used to sit in as a child, I feel like I have come home. I feel connected to my mom here, and although sometimes it's where my tears flow like an automatic release valve, at other times it's a comfort to my soul. It is so much more than just my religion, and I feel very fortunate that I have a place where I can go and feel deeply connected.

Even though my faith has helped me believe that those who go before us are in a "better place," it still does not mean that I want them to be there yet. After my mom died, I never considered seeking a medium. My mom had always shown me signs that she was with me. The continuing bonds I have shared with her are so strong. But after Brian's death, I was truly lost. I needed something else. I needed a chance to talk to my brother, even if all of this sounded crazy, so I scheduled an appointment anyway. Her first available appointment for a healing session was a few months out, at the end of August, and I took it. A few weeks before the appointment, I received a call saying that the appointment had to be rescheduled due to a conflict. The new appointment was now scheduled for October 1st, Brian's birthday. Did I mention that I don't believe in coincidences?

On the day of the appointment, I did not know what to expect, and I was a ball of anxiety. I prayed that I wasn't going to go to Hell and I also begged God to help me with some relief from my pain. By the time I arrived at Anysia's office, I'm pretty sure if you were standing next to me you could see my heart beating through my chest. But as soon as she walked up to her office door, I felt calmer. She had a beautiful and soothing presence about her. Once she unlocked the door and we walked in, she was immediately overcome. Tears filled her eyes. I could see her pain, and I wanted to know what was happening. "Your brother is here," she whispered. At that moment I needed to be reminded to breathe. "*Bri*," I could barely say his name, and the tears slowly started rolling down my face.

I hadn't told her too much before the session, and I really did not know how much she knew about me. She could tell that Brian had suffered in his death. The air was so heavy, it was palpable. She invited me to lay down on a table that looked like a massage table. My mind was racing, and my body was restless. I tried to get comfortable and center myself by observing the simplistic beauty of the room and breathing in the soothing scents of lavender and eucalyptus, one deep slow breath after another.

Her healing session began with a prayer, and I immediately felt at ease. The spiritual component was exactly what I needed to open myself to this moment and find a steady calm for myself. Then, Anysia began to share what Brian was saying to her, that he was so sorry for hurting all of us so deeply, and that he was especially sorry for the pain he was putting myself and my siblings through. He said he didn't mean to do it, but he had been hurting so badly, and he just missed Mommy so much. Brian was still just Mommy's baby, and his ache was too great to tolerate any longer. He shared that he still had some work to do, and some more people to help heal through his death, but he was *okay*, and I deeply felt that in the moment. I do not think my tears stopped during that entire conversation; it was a true cathartic release.

Connecting with Brian in this way was the start of my journey to heal after his death. When he was finished speaking through Anysia, she gently said, "Your mom is waiting." "*Mommy*," I cried. Honestly, I didn't know how much my heart could take. At that time, it had been over 15 years since my mom spoke to me. She told me how much she loved me and how proud she was of me. I had dreamt of hearing this validation from her so many times. She also told me that I had to stop fighting with Emily. *What?!* I blinked back my tears. *Oh no, you see me fighting with Emily*, I thought, and immediately felt ashamed. My mom continued, "You are a really good mother, Meaghan, but this behavior is not about her age, this is her personality, and you need to learn how to work with her or you will continue to butt heads. She is independent and bold and beautiful, and I am so proud of her too. Give her three choices, all choices that you are comfortable with, and then allow her to choose, empower her, and focus on your love." I couldn't believe that my mother had just given me parenting advice from Heaven through a medium. Later that night, when I told Jay what she had said about Emily, he responded, "Your mom is right." I smiled, and I nodded in agreement.

When Anysia and I were wrapping up the session, she had me sit for a while, holding some grounding stones, and recapped what had just happened. She said that I would likely feel tired for the rest of the day, and probably very emotional as well. It was a very powerful session, and even though I couldn't quite understand what I had just experienced, I knew that it was profound. As soon as I got in the car, I called Kerry. I needed to tell her in person what had just happened. I needed to tell her what Mommy and Brian had said, but I could not tell her in a text or over the phone.

Kerry told me to come over since all our kids were in school, and she happened to be home. With full-time jobs and five children between the two of us, time was a precious luxury. I couldn't remember the last time we had had two minutes alone together, let alone for two hours. I told her everything about the session and she believed me. She said she wanted to go herself, so a few weeks later she scheduled her own appointment. The first available appointment was January 20th, the anniversary of our mother's death. Did I mention that I don't believe in coincidences?!

Over the years, Anysia and I developed a very special friendship. I trusted her with some of my most intimate feelings of grief and vulnerability while she was helping me heal. She would always start the session by sharing a message that she received for the purpose and intention of that session. I could only ever hear Anysia's voice relaying these messages, but the tone and content always struck me in a deeply impactful way. Some of the intentions for my sessions included peace, healing, alignment, letting go, and clearing. She would also continue to connect with my family. I know it sounds crazy to some, but I honestly do not care. Our sessions always felt like a beautiful healing moment for my soul. Throughout the years, more of my family members had their own sessions with Anysia, and I referred her to countless friends as well. I am forever grateful to her for opening my mind to the idea that the next life is not that far away, and that if we allow ourselves to be open and our vibrations to be high, our spirits can not only guide us from up above, but alongside us as well. Truly believing and understanding this idea became transformative in my healing.

If you are interested, you can learn more about Anysia's work at *www.anysiakiel.com* and I also highly recommend her book, *Discovering the Medium Within.*

Reflection

Letter writing can be a very powerful tool at any point in time, but it is especially therapeutic when we are in grief.

Take this time to write a letter to your person (or people) that has died. Use this opportunity to tell them what is in your heart, what they meant to you, how your life has changed since they have been gone, and anything else that comes to your mind. This exercise may evoke a range of emotions, so please be patient with yourself.

Dear

Now try writing a letter to yourself, from your person who died. Think about what they would say to you. It may feel awkward at first, but I assure you, if you can get still enough, you will hear the words flow through you.

Dear

CHAPTER SEVEN

alchemizing pain into purpose

"If you can take this chaos and make it into art, then you, my dear, are an alchemist." —Nausicaa Twila

Sometimes people and places are planted right in front of you to guide you to your next step. If we were to zoom out on the big picture of our lives, the placement of those people may seem obvious. However, when we are zoomed in, living amid it all, it can be hard to see. It can sometimes take a while to realize why certain people, places, or things continue to show up again and again.

The first time I heard about Common Ground was at a fundraiser for the kids' school in early 2018. Common Ground is a grief center for children and teens who have lost parents and siblings. My initial thought was, *wow, how have I never heard of this?* And my second thought was, *I really wish this place was around for Brendan and Brian after Mommy died.* As I looked further into the organization, I discovered that there were volunteer opportunities available. I delved into their website and began following them on social media. But even though I felt drawn to their cause, I was still talking myself out of it. I told myself that I would not be capable of sitting in that kind of grief with children. Plus, to become a volunteer required 21 hours of mandatory facilitator training split up over two weekends, and at the time I was working full-time, and my children were nine and seven with active after school schedules. Ironically, it seems that sometimes the things we are supposed to do the most, we hold out against with great force. As Carl Jung, the incredibly brilliant Swiss psychiatrist simply puts it, "What you resist persists." And that it did.

After my mom died, I returned to school at the University of Scranton and continued with my business major without much thought about my future. By Christmas break of my sophomore year, I returned home for good, transferred schools and a few years later, I graduated with honors, as a Dean's Scholar from Georgian Court University with a B.S. in Business Administration, a concentration in Marketing, and a minor in Management.

Before the first worst day of my life, I had envisioned my post-college life quite differently. I imagined working in New York City, living in Hoboken or Jersey City, then eventually working my way up to a Manhattan apartment. I envisioned a big, bustling office environment, great shoes, delicious morning coffee, a nice paycheck, and Friday happy hours with my friends (yes, I envisioned my own *Sex in the City*). It had never occurred to me to reconsider my college major until I had already graduated and realized that there was no way in Hell I would leave my family to live and work in the city. I fought hard to come home from college, and I was not leaving again, as our family was very much still gluing back the shattered pieces.

Finding a job locally after college was a challenge. It was hard to find something that felt like the right fit. After almost a year of trying to find a steady job, while still waitressing and interviewing, Kerry told me about a jeweler that was looking for office help. Considering I knew nothing about jewelry, I did not have high expectations, but I went to the interview regardless. Much to my surprise, I was offered a full-time position almost immediately. I accepted and stayed for 18 years!

The first few years were pretty good. My boss, Joe, and I were basically a two man show, but it worked. He traveled a lot, and I would hold things down at the office. I was grateful to have a job that was consistent, and he took good care of me as an employee. It was mostly a wholesale operation, so I was able to use some of my business skills, while also building relationships with clients across the country. After a few years, we moved to a new location and opened a retail store. It was a great move for Joe and the company, and our staff grew to accommodate the new location. Over the years, I built beautiful friendships with Veronica, Laura, and Justine. They were incredibly supportive during some of my most challenging times, especially returning to work after the death of Brian and my dad.

Despite having a good job and being surrounded by coworkers who were like family, I always knew that I was meant to, and wanted to, do something else. I never envisioned staying as long as I did, but the more years that went by, the more difficult it felt to leave. My job became increasingly difficult after I had Shane and Emily; I hated commuting and leaving them for 10 hours a day. As they got a little older, I craved a job where I could create my own schedule so that I never had to miss a special school performance, sporting event, or have to call someone else to watch them when they were sick so I could go to work. My mom heart felt a longing to be more available for my children, and I also couldn't shake the feeling that I was not fulfilling my purpose. The internal struggle was unsettling.

It wasn't until after my father died that I knew I finally had to do something, as my thoughts would constantly go back to Father Michael's homily, encouraging us to answer the call on our hearts. I was deep into working full-time, raising kids, managing the apartments and overseeing the remodeling work, while also dealing with the many legal documents, taxes, potential malpractice suit, and getting our childhood home in order for the next rental season. My plate was OVERFLOWING. My grief was also overcoming me, and once again I didn't know how to process it. I felt like I was barely holding it together, and that was on a good day. One day I came across an interview with Father Richard Rohr, an American Franciscan priest and writer on spirituality, and he said, "If you don't transform your suffering, you will transmit it." Ouch, that hit hard. It was time to do *something,* and I knew I was ready.

Just a few months after hearing about Common Ground, and struggling through my father's unexpected death, I decided to sign up for the next facilitator training course. I reached out to Lynn, the Director and Founder of Common Ground, and registered. I wasn't sure how I would add this to my already hectic schedule, but I did it anyway. Lynn led and facilitated the training experience, which ended up being more like a personal retreat for me. I felt sad, I felt relief, and I felt **purpose**. My soul felt like it was on fire, and I knew after the first night of training that I had stepped into something that would become much more than a volunteer position. I was so excited, which I realize seems odd, considering I was training to be a facilitator at a grief center for children, but the irony was not lost on me.

One of the most important lessons I learned during that training session was about truth telling. It is so important to tell kids how their loved one died. When someone dies from an illness or an accident, we can explain it to a child in a way that feels honest, despite it still being massively unfair. But when someone dies from substance abuse, suicide, murder, or in some other tragic or unexpected way, it can be very difficult to share that truth. We also don't want to tarnish the memory of the person, especially if they had a good relationship. Parents and caregivers innocently try to protect children from the truth sometimes, but it does not help them in the long run. It's confusing and frustrating. This was something I struggled with since Brian's death. Shane and Emily were so young when he died, but I knew that eventually I would have to tell them the truth, and I wanted them to hear it from me first. How scary it must be for a child to think that a healthy 25-year-old could just die one morning.

Uncle Eddie said they used to call someone who died by suicide "dying of a broken heart." I tried to use this in my truth telling to soften it. A few weeks after the training, on a random car ride with Shane and Emily from one activity to the next, Shane, who was then 10 years old, asked a question that prompted me to tell him the truth about his uncle. While I did not get into the details of the suicide, I did tell them that Uncle Brian ended his own life. We spoke about Brian's grief from Grandma Joan's tragic death when he was a little boy and how his heart was hurting too much, regardless of the fact that he loved us all very much. We spoke about the importance of talking to other people when we are struggling and how everyone goes through hard times. It was a heavy conversation. I know hearing all of this made them sad, and then eventually mad, and then sad again. But that is grief in all its messiness. Over the years, Shane would write about his Uncle Brian's death. He even gave a speech on suicide in the 7th grade. He was not uncomfortable speaking about suicide and used his uncle's death as a way to raise awareness. I was so proud of how he was able to articulate this very serious and sensitive topic to his 12- and 13-year-old peers.

After the training, I felt lit up. Maybe my grief had a bigger purpose? I excitedly spoke to Jay about it, explaining that I'd never felt so alive in my life and that I knew this was something I needed to do for more than just a few hours a month. Jay was supportive and encouraged me to use the volunteer role to see what it would be like to work hands-on with the kids.

In the chilly early months of 2019, I began volunteering with a group of 6- to 12-year-olds, on Tuesday nights after a full day of work, and it was incredible. Their beauty in articulating grief through art and play was so impactful for me to witness. I thought I would drive home crying, but it was unexpectedly the opposite. It was an energy that is hard to put into words, and I knew that I wanted more of that feeling because I was finally understanding the call on my heart.

By the end of Spring 2019, my wheels were in motion, and I was not slowing down. After much research into various mental health career options, I made the decision to pursue a master's degree in counseling at Kean University. Kean had a satellite campus at Ocean County College, just ten minutes away from my house. OCC was where I spent my "transition" semester after my mom died. Never would I have imagined that I would be back on this campus almost 20 years later pursuing a completely different degree. Most of the classes would be in person on nights and weekends, but as the program progressed, I would likely have to travel to the Union campus, over an hour away, for some of the classes, because they weren't all offered locally. I did not like that idea, but I figured I'd cross that bridge when I got to it. The program required 60 credits consisting of classwork, practicum, and internships. I was still working at the jewelry store, plus I was still a mom, a wife, and was managing the rentals and responsibilities of our childhood home. But I had a greater purpose, and my "why" was tremendous.

I began courses that September. My first semester had me leave home every Saturday morning at 8:30, and I typically didn't get home until close to 4:00 in the afternoon. While I did not love leaving my family on a cozy Saturday morning, I could see something much greater in our future. I also would think of the saying,

"Nothing changes, if nothing changes." I was making *big* changes, and I was motivated, I was purposeful, and I knew I was exactly where I was meant to be, I could feel it. It felt steady and intentional, and I was proud to model this bold behavior to my children. I could see my future as a counselor and how choosing my hard now would ultimately create a better tomorrow for all of us.

My classmates became like family during that time and would affectionately refer to me as "Mama Meag." I was one of the older students in most of my classes, but I didn't mind. I wore the "Mom" badge with honor. I knew that what I lacked in being fresh out of undergrad (including the dreaded skills of APA-style paper writing), I made up for in life experience. That nudge of something *more* was finally quieting down.

In March 2020, the world shut down for Covid. I was only halfway through my second semester and, like everyone else, I wasn't sure what this would look like. How would I prioritize my family with virtual homeschooling and keep everyone healthy and safe and sane? Despite the uncertainty during Covid, our little family thrived in our bubble. The time together felt like a gift and a much-needed pause from our otherwise non-stop busy schedule that went seven days a week from morning till night. In the matter of a few weeks my classes all became virtual, and I was now an online student just like my kids. I didn't love it as much as in-person classes, but now I was able to take more classes per semester without having to commute to the Union campus. I did not know how long this opportunity would last, so it was at this point that I decided to become a part-time employee and become a full-time grad student to take advantage of the virtual classes. It was full steam ahead!

I knew that I wanted to be a counselor, but I wasn't sure exactly what kind of setting. Did I want to work in a school, or a clinic, or a private practice? The degree I was pursuing was Licensed Professional Counselor with the school counseling option, which meant that I would need to intern in a clinical setting as well as a school setting. My hope was that it would become clear to me where I was meant to be during the process.

My practicum and clinical internship experiences were insightful and informative. My first experience was at an outpatient behavioral health facility for a hospital. My supervisor, Sue, modeled sound counseling skills that I still use today, and seeing her in action inspired me. She exuded confidence and possessed a natural way of engaging with her clients. She showed me how much I could help others through the implementation of various therapeutic skills and techniques. Sue empowered me to trust my instincts and encouraged me when I doubted myself. The lessons I learned from her were invaluable. It was the first time I was able to have one-on-one sessions with clients, and I felt deeply connected to my purpose. I was intimidated to start seeing clients alone, but I quickly began building a rapport and discovering my own unique style while building my self-confidence. I also was able to participate in group sessions and found this to be a very powerful form of therapy.

During this time, I was simultaneously preparing to take my state licensing exam. I have never studied so hard for anything in my life. It is no exaggeration to say that for several months I was eating, breathing, and sleeping an exam prep guide called the "purple book." I also listened to the purple book companion CDs (because they did not have a digital component at that point) and downloaded apps that were quick study guides, and whenever I had a minute or two, I would do a quick, ten question quiz.

On the day of the exam, I drove to a testing center near Atlantic City, about an hour away from home. It was the closest option I had, and it was a torrential downpour! My windshield wipers could hardly keep up. I drove there listening to the CDs, knowing I should probably clear my head, but I couldn't help myself. When I got to the testing center, I tried to calm myself and prepare. I sat in my parked car for a few moments, taking several long deep breaths, breathing in through my nose, and out through my mouth. I prayed to God and everyone I knew in Heaven to help me through. I knew that I could not possibly have studied any harder, which gave me comfort, but also fear. The test cost a few hundred dollars, but with the mental stress it had put on me and my family, it may as well have been a few thousand dollars. I did *not* want to retake this exam. I was already taking so much time away from my family at this point. Knowing that I had studied so hard made me realize that if I did not pass, I wasn't sure what else I could possibly do to prepare if I had to take it again. So much for calming my nerves!

The test was hard and sometimes tricky. There were questions I felt *Yes, I know that!* but for others I thought, *I never even studied this, I have no idea*. I used my old SAT prep mindset and focused on the process of elimination whenever in doubt. When I completed the test, I felt relieved even though I would not know for two more months if I passed or failed. But I knew one thing, that I was not touching that purple book for the next two months. The day I received the email that I passed the exam, I cried.

Posts

meaghanhughes422

43 24

Liked by [illegible] others

meaghanhughes422 o weeks ago I drove to a testing center in pouring rain outside of AC to take my 4 hour national licensure exam. I have never ever ever studied so hard for anything in my life! My family witnessed me be completely neurotic and determined for two months 🤪 today I received the email that I PASSED my NCE!! Ahh!! 🎉🎉 I cried! I am so proud of me!

If someone would have told me 5 years ago this is where I would be, I would have never believed it!

This exam was HARD. Going to grad school at 40 is HARD. Sacrificing time with my family is HARD. But it is so WORTH it! It's never too late! The harder the challenge, the greater the reward 🩶

#counselorinthemaking #passion+purpose #enjoyingthejourney #almostthere #51creditsdown9togo

My Instagram post read:

> 6 weeks ago I drove to a testing center in pouring rain outside of AC to take my 4 hour national licensure exam. I have never ever ever studied so hard for anything in my life! My family witnessed me be completely neurotic and determined for two months 🤪 today I received the email that I PASSED my NCE!! Ahh!! 🎉🎉 I cried! I am so proud of me!
>
> If someone would have told me 5 years ago this is where I would be, I would have never believed it!
>
> This exam was HARD. Going to grad school at 40 is HARD. Sacrificing time with my family is HARD. But it is so WORTH it! It's never too late! The harder the challenge, the greater the reward 🖤 #counselorinthemaking #passion+purpose #enjoyingthejourney #almostthere #51creditsdown9togo

Shortly after receiving the news that I passed the exam, I completed my final days of practicum and internship at the outpatient facility. I was riding high and swiftly moving along in my program and personally growing leaps and bounds. There were plenty of days and nights when I felt burnt out, stressed, and overwhelmed, but I knew that I needed to keep moving forward because I was getting closer to the finish line.

In January 2022, I began the school counseling portion of my internship. This was my home stretch. I was assigned to work in a middle school from January to June. I would "walk" with my class at graduation in May and officially be conferred in August. My school counseling experience was a huge lesson for me. Anthony, the guidance counselor I was assigned to work with, instantly became a great friend. He welcomed me into his office three days a week, and I was his shadow. I observed his counseling skills when students appeared in his office in distress, I followed him to meetings and lunch duty and basically anywhere he needed to be in the building for six months. His style was different from mine, and yet we shared so much in common. I saw how he interacted with the students and how they responded to him, it clearly came very naturally for him. I valued being exposed to another perspective and learning new skills and ways of engaging. This experience was such a stark contrast to the clinical experience, which I really appreciated, and I felt like I had learned so much from both.

Even though I knew early on that a school environment was likely not the right fit for me, I learned so much during that internship and I gave it everything I had. Having had an inside experience in middle school would later help me in my own office, allowing me to better understand the current day-to-day experiences, dynamics, and culture that teens today are facing.

Having been the wife, daughter, sister, and friend of many teachers, I came into the school with the utmost respect for everyone in the building. After spending six months there, that appreciation grew. The work of counselors, administrators, teachers, secretaries, coaches, custodians, lunch aides, and everyone else within the building plays a crucial role in each student's life. But the time restraints of school counseling were not enough for me. I loved being there for the kids who needed it, but I wanted more. I wanted the hour. I wanted the door closed and I wanted to go deeper. Working in a school carries tremendous responsibility to help guide and navigate the students that come through the building. I will always appreciate that experience because it helped show me who I wanted to be and helped me realize that I wanted to work in private practice. Sometimes learning what you *don't* want leads you to exactly where you are supposed to be.

While I was preparing to apply for jobs at the end of my school year, I began to reflect on the many steps along the way that had gotten me to this point. I decided to send Lynn at Common Ground an email to thank her for inspiring me to go back to school and pursue my calling. Something about her story and the work she was doing helped me uncover something within myself, something that I had been searching for all along. For years and years, there was a call in my heart and a voice in my head: *You're meant to do more. This is not it.* The voice of my inner being is not loud, but boy is it persistent. The "responsible" (a.k.a. fearful) side of my brain would shush that with, *we have kids, and we have financial responsibilities, I have a good job, don't be selfish.* Maybe it was God, or maybe it was my intuition, or maybe it was my angels from above, but I knew it was right, and the day I started grad school, the voice stopped. I knew I was on the right path, so when I reached out to Lynn, I just wanted to say thank you and that "*I did it.*" After three years and tons of family time sacrificed, I was completing my master's and I felt like I had evolved into a stronger, more confident woman, and I appreciated the role she played, whether she realized it or not. Before signing off on the email, I asked if she knew anyone looking to hire counselors since she knew me and would likely know who a good fit would be.

Later that day, Lynn responded. She was so happy for me and so kind, then asked, "Do you remember Sonora? You two used to volunteer on the same night." Of course I remembered Sonora. Sonora had a beautiful energy and light about her, it was hard to forget. "Sonora is expanding her practice and moving to a new location in town. She is looking to bring on more therapists, and she said you should definitely contact her." *Wow*. My heart stopped. *Oh my gosh, what a great opportunity!*

I immediately reached out to Sonora, and we met the next week. It was so easy and natural. The office had such good energy, and the aura was soothing and peaceful. It was lovely to see her again and to see her in her element. I told her that my license should be coming through by the end of the summer, and she said that I could start as soon as I received it. I couldn't believe it. I dreamed of working in an office like this and now it was becoming my reality. Manifest much? I drove home with excitement and tears of gratitude. I said a special prayer of thanks for Common Ground. I went there with my own grief hoping to help others, but it ended up helping me more than I can express. I was reminded of the beautiful quote by Saint Francis of Assisi, "For it is in giving that we receive" and indeed, I did receive.

On September 14, 2022, on what would have been my dad's 77th birthday, I started working at the counseling center. This, of course, was no coincidence. I started with one client, and over the course of a few months my caseload grew and grew. I now see children and adults of all ages, individuals, couples, and families. I see many people in grief, people who struggle with anxiety and depression, people going through divorce and other major life transitions and challenges. Mostly, I see people just like me who are going through something HARD. It is an honor to work with people during their most difficult moments and help them discover their own purpose and healing.

My work is extremely meaningful, and I am incredibly thankful. It is not easy, but I know with every fiber of my being that I am exactly where I am supposed to be. Every day one of the mantras I say, before I even get out of bed in the morning, is "Thank you" and the other is "Help me help others, help me help myself." I know that without a doubt, those two things are connected in the most profound way.

Reflection

Take a few moments to unpack the following questions to help you discover your own unique purpose.

What is your purpose?

We are not limited to one purpose in our lifetime. In fact, different seasons in our life can introduce new versions of ourselves, and what was once so important to us may not be now. So what is your purpose in this moment in time, as you are moving through your grief? Ask yourself, how can I be living a more purposeful life? When we allow ourselves to observe the moments in our lives when we are thriving, when we simply cannot explain the way we just "know", it starts to become more clear.

This exercise may take some time, so don't rush it. Keep in mind, this does not need to make sense to anyone else. Envision your truest self and imagine you could not fail. Think about the people, things, times, and places that make your soul come alive. ***Who*** makes you feel this way? ***What*** are you doing when you feel like the best and most authentic version of yourself? ***When*** are you feeling this way? ***Where*** are you?

Who?

What?

When?

Where?

Once you answer your who, what, when and where, go back and ask yourself **Why?** to each prompt.

Why does this person make me feel this way?

Why does this particular thing make me feel this way?

Why is this timing meaningful?

Why is this place important to me?

There is so much power in uncovering the ***why***, and you can peel back the onion as many layers as you need to feel content with your response.

Something else to think about . . .

Is there a volunteer opportunity that could allow you to experience something purposeful on a deeper level or a training or class you can take to further your meaningful connection to your own purpose? I encourage you to take the first step, however small it is, baby steps are still steps, and small action has the power to create momentum.

CHAPTER EIGHT

lessons i've learned and discovered along the way

Lesson 1:

My trauma is not their trauma

I am not afraid to die, but I am afraid to leave my children without a mother. This is *my* trauma, the trauma that I sadly cast on my children, even in the most beautiful moments. Moments when I am trying to capture a quick picture because I want it to live forever in my mind. My heart is full when the four of us are together, and when Triton is with us too, it is a perfect 10. Whether we are taking a ride on the boat or snuggling on the couch watching one of our shows, it is all pure joy for me. And then my mind goes there. I want to live for them. I don't want them to know the pain of living without a mother. I don't want them to know the pain I still live with, and yet I want to show them that life can still be beautiful and filled with so much love. Both can be true. Emotional ambivalence is a feeling I know like the back of my hand.

In just a few short years, Shane will be the age I was when our mother was tragically taken from us. I didn't realize how young I was at the time. I thought 18 was *so* old, certainly much older than my siblings who were lined up on the stairs that dreadful January morning. I was wrong. I had so much responsibility instantaneously, and I leaped into the role without hesitation. I now see that I was *just a girl*. I was forever changed after my mother's death. Losing her has been a constant theme surrounding everything in my life, but it also ignited the flame of desire to create meaning out of all of this, out of, as famed poet Mary Oliver so poignantly describes, "our one wild and precious life".

I find myself living at times like we, myself and my children, only have a few years left together. The age of 18 is not just the age when my children will go off to college, 18 is also the age I was the last time I ever saw my mother. Most parents are keenly aware of the time slipping away before their children graduate high school and are preparing to take the next step in their journey, whatever that may be. And while that has already begun consuming my thoughts, more often than I would like, my mind is also telling me a much darker story, one where *my time* is almost up. It's really hard not to think about these scenarios, and as a therapist I am keenly aware of how unhelpful these thoughts can be. But I am also human. I know that this is not their reality. I pray that I will be here for them to a ripe old age, and if I am, I will know that every single day is a privilege. But we don't know, none of us know for sure, which is why it is so important to live our lives with love and purpose and to be intentional with our choices. We need to make the most of each day, and to fill our hearts with gratitude for what we have right at this very moment. We are each on our own journey, learning lessons along the way, making mistakes, wishing we could go back and get a redo. But all we can do is pick ourselves up, learn from it, and try again. We do not just *go* through the motions of grief, we *grow* through the grief.

That's exactly what I had to do on a late Sunday afternoon in the fall of 2023. We were all on the boat, Triton too, taking a cruise.

It had been a while since we were able to find an hour of family time amidst our non-stop calendar of scheduled practices, games, and social events. I knew these nights were becoming more and more infrequent as the kids were getting older, so I was soaking it in. The sky was putting on its glorious show, and the water was reflecting every light with true majestic beauty. And then, all of a sudden, I was crying and, somehow, it led to an argument. I spoiled the moment. Damn grief. Sometimes I got so overwhelmed with my emotions that I unintentionally pushed too hard on my children. My thoughts consumed me in that moment, and I went to the dark side, imagining not being here, you know, just in case I died in a couple of years. I made a passive aggressive comment about dying, and before I knew it, we were fighting, and I could feel everyone's frustration on how I just ruined the day. I instantly regretted it. I really can't stand myself in these moments. I hate being morbid or considered a martyr, it is a part of me that I try very hard to work through, and a part that I try to heal so that I do not project that onto them. I just want them to know how precious our time together is, but until one experiences such a loss, you cannot truly know. And so, I cannot blame them for not understanding my perspective, and I also should not burden them with impending doom and gloom. It's a delicate dance that is best performed when I slow down enough to remind myself that this grief is not theirs to carry.

A little later that night, after we got home, I approached Shane. I knew he was frustrated with how I reacted, and I was too. I hugged him with all my might, and he hugged me back, a really strong hug, and I apologized and told him how sorry I was for the way I acted. One of the most important things I try to show my children is that when I screw up or when I'm wrong, you better believe I will own it. I told him that the argument was a *me* thing and not a *him* thing. I told him that my pain is not his, and I am constantly working on managing these emotions. I also reminded him that my love is unconditional and endless, whether I am here or not. I learned that after my mom died. A mother's love truly knows no bounds, has no earthly restrictions. If you need her, she will find you, and she will let you know she is still with you. Shane graciously accepted my apology that night, and I was so grateful.

Lesson 2

What I believed as a child: *Sensitivity is my weakness.*
What I believe as an adult: *Sensitivity is my superpower.*
"It's better to feel pain than nothing at all." —Lumineers

Growing up, I was always told that I was sensitive. I'm not sure who told me this, but eventually I started telling myself that too. I knew that I cried easily. I could feel tears forming and a lump in my throat at the drop of a hat. I hated getting in trouble or having anyone mad at me or not liking me. In my mind, sensitivity was a weakness, and therefore I was weak. It wouldn't be until much later in my life that I realized sensitivity was my superpower. I began to understand this profoundly when I was volunteering at Common Ground. I recognized that this thing that I had so vehemently disliked about myself was actually one of my most important traits. I could see it enabled me to draw others near in the most endearing way. It was part of the discovery process in finding my purpose, recognizing that part of myself as a strength, instead of a weakness. It helped me rewrite the narrative that I had lived by. I wasn't weak, I was strong, and I felt big feelings. I still feel big feelings, for myself and for others. My empathy and compassion are through the roof. I am drawn to people struggling. I walk towards, I don't walk away. It is just a part of me. I feel deeply and it's almost as if I can feel what the other person is feeling. This helps me connect to, and become in tune with, that person, placing my own opinions or assumptions on the shelf. It's a trait that now serves me daily in my relationships with my husband, my children, my friends, my siblings, and my clients. I am proud of myself for embracing my sensitivity and that I use it for good.

But this sensitivity can still feel a little over-the-top sometimes. Thankfully, those who love me have embraced it. Sometimes we will be watching a movie or TV show, and something tragic occurs or someone dies, or there is just a pull on your heart strings commercial, and almost instantly my kids check on me. "Are you okay, Mom?" Or they don't say anything and just hug me, or reach out their hand, and in that moment, I am more than okay, because even though they may not feel the same big emotion I am experiencing, they are sensitive enough as humans to be in touch with someone else's and that makes me really proud. So yeah, it took decades to understand, but sensitivity is my superpower. What is yours?

Lesson 3

Movement is a mood booster

"I can't help you, you should try yoga," was what my therapist told me after Brian died. I had been seeing her for a few months, spilling my soul, and here she was telling me to try yoga. *What the fuck?* I was pissed. *Maybe she couldn't help me. Maybe I was helpless?* I felt awful leaving that session. I also always felt uncomfortable and judged somehow because she was always taking notes, and she never smiled. *Did she even like me? Why do I care so much?* And now she seemed done with me.

I now know that we weren't a great fit, *and* I still had to move through my grief. I say this because if you've had a similar experience, or something just didn't sit right with a therapist, try and try again. We're all uniquely human, so we will each connect completely differently. Don't let a bad experience prohibit you from finding a therapist you really connect with. When the therapeutic relationship is working well, it can be powerful and healing. While at the time I had no idea that I would eventually become a therapist, I learned some valuable lessons. I never use a clipboard in my office, and I do not take notes during a session. Many therapists take notes throughout their sessions, and it works well. I think my discomfort from the experience I had stayed with me, and so for me, it's a no. I try, from the first session, to disarm my clients by being kind, and I smile. I want them to feel seen, heard, supported, and understood during the session, and after they leave. I want them to continue to carry that feeling into the week ahead and use it as a support to work through whatever challenges they are facing. I do not pretend to be superior, or have it all figured out myself, but I've been through my share of struggles, and I continue to heal and move forward, so I can confidently say, I do practice what I preach.

Ironically enough, years later, I did come to find yoga as a major release. Throughout the years I would go with friends on and off, more as a social excuse, never consistently. Then in 2021, I embraced hot yoga. I consistently went every Friday for months, usually alone. I run and bike and strength train throughout the week because I like to switch it up, but I am terrible at stretching. When my workout is done, I am done. It's a terrible habit, and I can feel the effects creeping into my 40+ year old body. At first, I said I used yoga as my stretch time, except it was probably the hardest workout I would do all week. I was a fan of the 90 minute, 100 degrees+ class. It was just as much a mental workout as it was a physical one, and I would be drenched after every class. It felt amazing. It forced me to get quiet in my mind and appreciate my body in a new way. When the summer hit, Fridays became our family beach day, so yoga took a back seat. Family time trumps most things, and as I mentioned, it's getting increasingly harder to make it work. But I do try to go back to it whenever I can. I hope to make it a consistent part of my weekly routine again because I know it really made a difference for me.

Running also became a part of my healing journey, becoming quite therapeutic over the years. It is hard, but I am addicted to the runner's high, and the healing that emerges through my runs is unlike anything else that I do. Running allows me to experience the best mental clarity. Running along the bay, or on the boardwalk, breathing in the salty air and experiencing the beauty of the natural landscape all around while the birds are singing their songs all fuel my soul, not to mention the endorphins pumping throughout my body, which can feel deeply euphoric. Sometimes I cry, sometimes I rock out and dance to whatever music is playing in my ears, but no matter what, I always end up feeling better than when I started.

I came from a family of competitive runners, and I ran here and there growing up, but I was not one of them. I eventually figured out how good it was for me to get out of my head and hit the pavement. After Shane was born, I began running with him and Kai, while pushing the stroller. Sometimes after work, even though I was tired, I would put the stroller in the car and meet my girlfriend Michelle on the boardwalk and we would push strollers and run together, stopping briefly to pick up a sippy cup that one of the kids threw or sprinkle a few more snacks on the tray. Michelle has always been a great accountability partner and helped me push through when I probably would have rather been on the couch after a long day. Once Emily came along, I had to trade in my single Bob jogging stroller for a double. It was significantly heavier and sometimes extra challenging to push, plus there was Kai, but I kept going, wanting them outside in the fresh air as much as possible. I don't know if I realized it at the time, but I do know now that I was modeling an important life habit. Mommy was moving. I began to realize just how important the mind-body connection truly is, and the way I felt mentally after a run was always so much lighter.

Bessel van der Kolk, MD shares this message and understanding of how profoundly connected our mind and body are in his book, *The Body Keeps the Score.* Bessel says, "Trauma comes back as a reaction, not a memory." I remember reading that and thinking, *Wow, that explains a lot.* Understanding this powerful concept allows us to more intimately understand our physical sensations or reactions, and it can be a reminder to first give ourselves some grace, and then gently move our bodies to release built up fear, tension, and anxiety swirling just beneath the surface.

While we know the obvious benefits of movement for our physical health, the psychological benefits are also extensive. Moving our body leads to the release of endorphins, the feel-good hormones, which in turn reduces our cortisol and stress levels. Movement also boosts energy levels, which often leads to improved mood and improved sense of self. In addition, exercise can also lead to better sleep at night, and who does not want to sleep better?

Jay took up running as well over the years. We started signing up for local 5Ks and appreciated the weekends when we could share the stroller pushing during our runs. After Brian died, Jay and I, along with GK and her husband, Kevin, and Jen, a childhood friend of hers, did a 26-mile run medley, the miles broken up amongst the team. My leg of the run took me over the Point Pleasant bridge into Manasquan where I work today. We ran a combined 26 miles for Brian the year that would have been his 26th birthday.

As the years went on, and the stroller days were behind us, we encouraged Shane and Emily to join us on our runs. They resisted most of the time, but occasionally they would come. It wasn't until seventh grade that Shane started to realize that he might be onto something with running. In November of 2021, we did our first Suicide Survivors Day 5K and Shane crushed it! We were so proud of him, and he was really surprised and excited by his time. That race gave him a new-found confidence for running, and after that point, he just kept getting stronger and faster.

That same day, Emily, who was in fifth grade at the time, and I ran the same race, but had quite a different experience. She started off fast and then quickly slowed down. I kept pushing her, *come on, come on!* I didn't want to stop; I wanted to run. I was so inspired by the other survivors running, and my adrenaline was pumping. But then she just stopped, saying that she was tired and her legs hurt. She was crying and she was mad. I started to walk with her, then I would jog, and then I would stop, and then I finally woke up. *What am I doing? Why are we even here*? I grabbed Emily's hand and told her that I would walk every step of the way with her and that I was so sorry for acting the way I did. We were there for Uncle Brian, her godfather, and he would not have been happy that I was pushing her like that. We hugged and started walking hand-in-hand. Thank God for apologies and owning them in the moment! After a few steps, Emily said, "I want to run again." I said, "Are you sure?" She responded, "Yup," and I said, "Okay, I'll be right behind you." We ran through the finish line a few minutes later, and the pride I had for her that day was enormous. While I could've beaten myself up for how I acted during the first half of the race, I instead was proud of myself too. I showed up for her. I hope the second half is what she will remember as well.

Shane went on to run for his high school team, striving to constantly push to his maximum effort, and going on casual seven mile runs like it's no big deal. Emily ran for her middle school cross-country and track teams, and went on to run indoor track in high school. But truth be told, soccer is her first love. Jay and I both still run, for our physical and mental health. We sign up for local 5Ks when we can fit them in. We started running for physical health and so much more has benefitted as a result. I couldn't be prouder that somewhere along the line our kids picked this up too. Yes, running can be hard on your body, cue hot yoga. And when I do not have the run in me, which seems to be more frequent than not the older I get, I take a brisk walk, which for me is a very similar pace. I pop in some Air Pods and listen to a podcast or a book on Audible, and I get connected to my breath. The pace of my walk increases and before I know it, my heart rate is up and I'm starting to sweat. I know that moving, even slowly, is still better than not moving at all. Moving your body is key to moving through any sort of trouble, grief, anxiety, or stress. We are made up of energy and that energy needs to go somewhere. If you can release it through a sweaty workout, it is quite an endorphin reward.

Maybe running and yoga are not your things, no problem. I encourage you to find your thing. It could be walking, or hiking, or biking, or surfing, or paddle boarding, or skateboarding, or snowboarding or skiing, or golfing, or playing tennis, or pickle ball, or shaking your groove thing at Zumba, or maybe it's mowing the lawn. You'll know when you've tapped into it because you will feel it, your mood will get its natural boost, and then you will crave more of that good feeling. It's important to remember though, that just because you find your thing, it does not guarantee that you will always be motivated to do the thing. The key is once you plan to move your body, do not wait too long to start, because sometimes we can talk ourselves out of it before we even begin, coming up with a million and one excuses and distractions. I know this all too well from my own experiences. Try to close the gap of time as much as possible between thinking about doing something and actually doing it. The less time you spend pondering, the more likely you will do the thing. And set yourself up for success. Find an accountability partner, sign up for a class the night before, or even just keep your sneakers and workout clothes next to your bed. Usually, the motivation doesn't kick in for me until I'm halfway through a workout, but I know that it does come eventually, so I push myself to get started, even when I don't want to, which is usually more times than not. The mental and physical reward is always greater than the resistance.

Lesson 4

Find your sign, or let it find you

In the days following my mother's burial, Erin and her mom came to pick me up for a few hours to get me out of the house. Having still been in the early stages of their own grief, I really appreciated the time spent together. They asked me where I wanted to go, and I requested, "*Please take me to the cemetery*." I wanted to go back so desperately. It was still January, the ground was frozen, and the dirt over top where her casket lay was still very fresh. We wouldn't have a headstone for a few months. I remember being very numb in that moment and feeling so lost. When we got back to the car, Erin's mom shared that after Doug passed, just one year prior, she discovered that rainbows became a symbol to let her know that her son was nearby. A rainbow in the sky was the best option, but sometimes it was a rainbow in a painting or one on a t-shirt. She encouraged me to think of something that really resonated with me that I could use as a sign that my mom was showing up. I stared out the window, intently thinking. I loved the rainbow idea, but I needed my own thing. *What could my sign be*? I thought back to the many paper napkins my mom would write on and put in our lunchboxes, and I remembered the smiley face she would always draw. Have a ☺ Monday XOXO, Mommy. She drew a smiley face on all the tests she graded for school and on the back-to-school notes she would leave on my desk. I said, "I think I'm going to make mine smiley faces." Not two seconds later, the car passing us on the other side of the road had two giant smiley face headlights. We all took a collective gasp, and it sealed the deal for me. That would be my sign. Since that day, I have found them everywhere, some in unusual or unexpected places. I have had quite the collection of smiley face items, from boxer briefs pajamas that my dad bought for me, to an antenna ball that my friend Nick put on my car one day. Yes, it looked silly, and I am not a car decor person, but it brought me comfort. After all these years I still see smiley faces everywhere, and it always feels like a hello from Heaven. I encourage you to find your sign. Find something that resonates and then allow it to find you. Your sign can provide comfort, especially in the early stages of your grief and allow you to feel a special connection to your loved one each time it appears.

Lesson 5

Recognize your angels on Earth

Besides Jay, Shane, and Emily, few people in my life have impacted me in the profound way that my Aunt Gail, Uncle Eddie, and my cousin, Denise, have. Since I was a young girl, Aunt Gail served as an important role model and a second mother figure. Uncle Eddie's words, texts, emails, and just the way he makes me feel, offer such comfort and compassion. I wish I could bottle it up. Denise has shown me how to be resilient and how to be the best mother, while not having our own mothers to physically guide or help us. Over time, I began to see her as the kind of friend I could confide in and feel completely myself with. I also don't find it surprising that the three people outside of my immediate family who acted, and continue to act, as my angels on Earth, are all an extension of my mother. Uncle Eddie was my mom's older brother, Aunt Gail was my mom's best friend, and Denise was my mother's niece, her sister, Katherine's oldest daughter.

Aunt Gail was a high-powered businesswoman, and I have looked up to her since I was a little girl. She was one of the main reasons I became a business major in college. It wasn't just that she worked in New York City and had fancy suits, it was also because she worked hard all week and then she and her husband, Uncle Big Ed, drove down every Friday night to spend the weekend at our house on a pullout couch. Aunt Gail was fun, and she was able to decompress on the weekends in the middle of all our never-ending chaos. Aunt Gail and Uncle Big Ed did not have kids of their own, but they had us. I'm sure that they were happy to go home to peace and quiet on Sunday nights, but while they were here, they often acted like bigger kids than us. Gail was my mom's best friend who was there for her after the sudden loss of my mom's sister, Katherine. For many years, until they eventually built a home down the shore, Aunt Gail and Uncle Big Ed were our weekend house guests. Friday nights were always pizza nights, then on Saturdays, Gail and my mom would cook a great meal, and finally on Sunday mornings we all attended church and then came back home and enjoyed bagels and crumb buns before they would head back home for the week.

Gail is also my godmother, and then I later asked her to be my Confirmation sponsor. I always felt a strong connection to her, and even when she put me in my place for talking back to my mom, I respected that. She fiercely had my mom's back always; their friendship was a true sisterhood.

After my mom died, a part of Gail died too. Throughout her heartache, she never once abandoned us. She stepped up whenever and wherever she could. Talking about my mom too much can be quite painful for her, but she does. She hosted my bridal party the morning of my wedding and was a source of calm for me that day. She was also a huge supporter of me going back to school and pursuing a lofty career change. She strongly supported and encouraged me to complete this book, while being a go-to resource for me about events that occurred when I was too little to remember or before I was born. I've always appreciated her role in my life, and I know I would not be who I am today without the love, encouragement, and consistency she has provided me for over 40 years.

My family visited Aunt Gail and Uncle Big Ed at their home in Marco Island, Florida during our spring break in 2024. They had become snowbirds over the years and really fell in love with this beautiful beach and fishing town. It was our first time there and it ended up being an unforgettable trip. GK, Kevin and their girls, Annabelle, Amelia, Kaitlin and Kasey, as well as Brendan and Amy and baby Brendan were there too. Gail and Ed were so happy to host us all in their slice of paradise. It was the first time in as long as I could remember that we were able to spend several days in a row together, reminiscing, eating and drinking, and enjoying each other's company. It brought back many memories of days long ago, and we created some very special new memories too.

Throughout 2024, Uncle Big Ed began feeling increasingly unwell and losing significant weight. He went from doctor to doctor in Florida to New Jersey and back to Florida again. After months of going in circles, he was finally diagnosed with pancreatic cancer. In January 2025, he began an intensive chemotherapy treatment plan. Not knowing exactly what the future months would bring, I felt it was important to return to Florida to offer encouragement to Big

Ed and to be a source of love and support for Aunt Gail, as she had been a sturdy rock for him during this time.

So, my family returned for a brief visit in April 2025, and we enjoyed more meals, laughter, and conversations. Despite enduring so many rounds of chemotherapy treatment at this point, Uncle Big Ed really rallied on the days that we were there and made the most of our visit. Although we could not see into the future, we knew the journey ahead would not be an easy one. Once the chemo treatment concluded, he would have to begin intensive radiation. We never really know how many opportunities we will get to spend time with the people we love. Whenever it is possible, take the trip, I am so glad that we did.

Only a few short months later, in July of 2025, while undergoing scheduled tests and scans to prepare for the next part of his treatment, it was revealed that Uncle Big Ed had developed pneumonia. His symptoms increased at a rapid pace, and he was hospitalized immediately, as he was experiencing labored breathing. A scan of his lungs revealed a very thick mucus that was not clearing up with the medications they were administering. He was put on oxygen and within a few days was moved to ICU where he needed to be put on a ventilator to perform a bronchoscopy, the only option to attempt to clear his lungs at this point.

It was at that point that I decided I needed to return to Florida to be with Aunt Gail and say goodbye to Uncle Big Ed. Having had to take my Dad off the ventilator and say farewell in that horrific way, I just knew she could not be alone for that. I flew down Wednesday, July 30 and took an Uber straight to the ICU when I landed in the late afternoon. I hardly recognized the man in the bed. Aunt Gail's first words were, "I'm so glad you didn't listen to me, and you came anyway." Ed was in bad shape, and the rest of his organs were now beginning to fail too. The following day, Uncle Big Ed would be taken off the ventilator. Gail's niece and nephew Brendan and Meaghan also flew down to Florida and joined us as we prayed and cried and said our final goodbyes. He passed peacefully not long after they removed the ventilator.

Later that evening, after numerous airline delays, my sister, Gail Katherine, and my brother, Brendan, arrived in Florida to be with Aunt Gail too. The following few days were filled with tears and reminiscing, planning services and helping Aunt Gail step into a chapter of life without her Big Ed.

In June of 1989, Cher released "If I Could Turn Back Time." This is one of those childhood memories that stands out clearly in my mind. I can envision us driving down the road in their Chevy Blazer, and every time this song came on the radio that summer, Gail and I would sing loudly. I loved it, and truly, if I could turn back time to just one of those Friday pizza nights, laughing and being so young and carefree, having my entire family alive and under one roof, I would do it in a heartbeat, and I have no doubt, everyone else would too.

Acknowledging Uncle Eddie's role in my life gives me a lump in my throat. Throughout my entire life he has been someone who has shown me love in an incredibly profound way. As a little girl, I loved playing with his trains and getting cozy by his fires. (He can still make a great fire.) As I got a little older, I enjoyed his delicious cocktails and appreciated his need to find the appropriate glass to drink a specific beer. (It really does matter!) But the thing that always struck me the most was his ability to put his love into words. Some people say things like, "I don't have the words to express this," or "I can't even put it into words," but not Uncle Eddie. His way with words is his superpower. In college, that first semester before my mom died, he sent me a little handwritten note with a $20 bill telling me to have a great weekend. After my mom died, his letters, emails, and texts would become so much more important and meaningful. I remember looking at him and thinking, *Wow, you have lost both of your sisters and both of your parents, how are you even still standing?*

Remember when I mentioned earlier how Mommy and Uncle Eddie made a great sibling team? They really did and I know that her death also gutted him to the core. But he did not let this inhibit him from being there for us. Every birthday, anniversary, and Mother's Day, he would send a note, often in the form of a prayer, like this:

> *"Today Joan, as we remember your loss, it hurts as much today as it did twenty years ago. We take comfort knowing and believing you're still by our side. Your memory is alive, and it burns in all of us as strong as ever. Your life is an example we cherish and in our own humble ways try to emulate. Often failing but knowing you're there rooting us on and giving us an A for effort.*
> *We love you, Joan."*

Part of Uncle Eddie's glow is his strong faith. I love when he comes to Mass, and I am serving the Eucharist, and I see him switch lines just so he can receive from me. Every time that happens, my heart is literally smiling. After Brian died, there he was again, comforting us with words that came so naturally to him. I hung onto every word so intently, allowing it to comfort me and heal me any way possible.

> *"Brian,*
> *Your short life left us with an unexpected burden we were not prepared to handle. Wish you had known the joy you brought to all of us that we so miss. Knowing you are with Mommy heals our hearts but not our wounds. We will always love you Brian and tell Mommy to pray for us to give us strength.*
> *Uncle Eddie"*

Uncle Eddie is such a kind and gentle man. He's smart and funny and loves to host a crowd, mostly because he loves to have as many of his family members under one roof as possible. I love to learn and listen to stories about his childhood and hear more about my mom and her sister and my grandparents. He always reminds us on Veteran's Day about the greatest generation and his father, my grandfather, who was highly decorated for his service to our country.

Uncle Eddie has shown me resilience and an unwavering faith through the darkest of times. He has modeled it so genuinely, and I continue to absorb the goodness in his aura whenever I am in his presence. He is a true blessing in my life and without a doubt, one of my angels here on earth.

My cousin Denise and I are naturally bonded, having spent most of our lives living without our mothers. But the bond that really connected me the most to Denise was watching her raise her incredible three, now adult, children without a mother here to guide, support, and lean on. Denise modeled this kind of motherhood for me, Kerry, and Gail Katherine in the most beautiful way. Now, being able to watch her cherish and dote on her grandchildren is next level. She has now become the grandmother she had longed for her own children to have.

Maybe it's her cool and calm disposition, or the way that she can laugh at us or normalize our not so normal situation. Maybe it's the way she validates my feelings, but I truly value my relationship with Denise. She also is fun and funny and a great conversationalist. She shows up often and checks in, and I try to do the same for her.

Denise disarms me in a way that makes me feel like I'm not a terrible mom when I'm having one of those days, and she deeply understands me. She can relate when I feel like life is not fair. I think about how lucky others are who are able to grow into adulthood with their mothers. Denise just gets it, and we can speak to each other freely in this way without feeling like we will offend each other or make the other person feel uncomfortable. It's refreshing and honest and a true gift to be seen and heard and understood.

Recently, something happened and I was bawling my eyes out. I needed to regroup, and I knew I needed to talk to someone to help calm me down. Without hesitation, I called Denise, sniffling and struggling to get the words out. She listened and told me that she was so glad I called. As her tears caught up with mine, we talked and reconnected. By the end of the conversation, I had collected myself and was able to face the day. The call was short, but the connection was deep, and I felt immense gratitude to have someone like this in my life.

These are a few of my very special angels on earth. When you think about your own life, who is popping into your mind right now? Who is that person or people who has etched themselves into your soul in the most beautiful way? I pray that you have at least one person like this in your life, and if you do, I encourage you to let them know now. Call them, text them, or send them a letter. Do not wait until they are gone to memorialize them. Let them know now how much you appreciate the role they've had in your life and then look around again because you may very well be someone else's angel here on Earth.

Lesson 6

Keeping them alive with continuing bonds

During the summer of 2025, I attended a virtual workshop led by Dr. Erica Sirrine, a Licensed Clinical Social Worker and Thanatologist. Her presentation was captivating as she had such an eloquent and relatable way with her words. She emphasized the need for, and importance of, implementing "continuing bonds" after death. Dr. Sirrine shared on her website, *HopeandGrief.com*, "Humans are created for connection, and our daily lives revolve around the intimate attachments we form. Death has the power to separate us from our loved ones physically, but it does not sever our emotional connections or bonds to them. Our love remains."

In 1917, Sigmund Freud defined mourning as severing from an object that no longer exists, essentially stating that we, as mourners, should simply "get over it" when someone dies. It was not until 1920, when his beloved daughter Sophie, died from the Spanish flu, that he completely changed his stance. Freud later went on to share that when someone we love dies, the pain and loss that we feel is necessary to "perpetuate that love which we do not want to relinquish."

Over the years I have come to believe that if it makes you feel good, and it's not hurting anyone else, do it. I try to incorporate continuing bonds with my mom, my dad and Brian into my daily life whenever I can. And I try to carry on traditions that hold a special place in my heart.

My coffee pot is set to brew every morning at 6:13 AM, my mom's birthday. It's a simple gesture that makes me happy. At Christmas time, we go to Del's Farm Market to seek out the perfect tree, just like I did with my parents. At Thanksgiving dinner, we say our prayers and then have a toast with Manischewitz, which was a tradition my mom carried on from her own parents. On Christmas Eve, the only gift Shane and Emily receive from us are matching Christmas jammies (Jay and I join in on this tradition too, because who doesn't love Christmas jammies?!). Growing up, that was the one gift my siblings and I received on Christmas Eve, and I was always excited to receive it!

On the last Thanksgiving that Brian was alive, he brought over a homemade spiked apple cider in a big pot. He said he had been simmering it all morning, and the aroma of cinnamon, nutmeg and cloves filled the air. I could tell he was proud of his concoction, and it was quite delicious. He took a picture of me holding Emily asleep in my arms, with the special cocktail in hand, posted to Instagram and captioned it "*Thankful for family*". I forgot to return that pot, and I am so glad that I still have it. To this day I use it all the time. I especially love to make sauce in it, and every time I use it, I think of Brian and that special moment we shared.

Many things remind me of my dad, and I always feel like I know where to find him when I am missing him. Whenever a storm is coming, I can't help but think of my dad. Whether it was a Nor'easter or a blizzard, he was invested, and The Weather Channel would be his lifeline. Every time Jay and I go to The Crab's Claw, a favorite local watering hole, we can't help but feel his presence. From the hand crafted buoy he made that hangs from the bar, to the smell of clam chowder and old bay seasoning, to the conversations around us from other old timers, I feel him close by. Whenever we are cruising on the bay and catching an epic sunset, I feel him in the beauty of the sky. And even though the stress of preparing our childhood home for our next rental season can be overwhelming, I always feel my dad's presence there, and I will often talk to him out loud. The comfort of that home, and his wood working and craftsmanship proudly displayed in and around the house, will always feel like Daddy to me.

Reflection

I think it is fair to say that we can learn a considerable amount from our own grief, the good and the ugly, I know I have. Although we did not ask for our eyes to be opened in this way, we certainly cannot view life as it was before. Here are some more prompts to help you reflect and process.

What lessons have you learned during your grief journey?

What do you wish other people (your family, friends, coworkers) knew about your grief?

We often talk about who we were before our person died and who we are after. How have you changed before and after?

What is your superpower, that unique gift that you possess and that shines brightly to those around you?

What type of physical movement are you already doing or what can you implement to boost your mood?

Who are your angels on earth and how have they impacted your life?

CHAPTER NINE

triggers + glimmers

While waitressing during the summer after my mom died in 2000, I remember experiencing a crippling feeling of overwhelming sadness while serving a young new mom who had a baby nestled in a stroller and her mom, who was proudly doting on her grandchild. *Wow, three generations, how special,* I thought. I went to the bathroom and cried . . . hard. I was so jealous in that moment. It felt so unfair that I would never get to experience my mom with me and the children I hoped to have one day. I was only 19, but I knew this pain deeply. Even though I didn't fully understand it at the time, this was one of my earliest triggers that I vividly remember. It's not that I wasn't happy for their relationship, in fact I admired it, *and* I longed for it, and to be completely honest, this particular image of a woman with her own children and her mother in tow, still stings at times, 25 years later.

Not too long ago, Emily and I went out for lunch, and it seemed that the majority of the restaurant was filled with women around my age and their moms. I caught myself welling up in that moment. I took a breath, looked at Emily and said, "I am so grateful to be here with you right now." We cannot always control what emotions come up for us, but we can control how we respond to them, so in that moment I chose gratitude for my daughter, and I envisioned a day when we could be sitting there with her children. This has not always come so easy for me, I have worked very hard over the years to look for the joy through the sadness, and I will continue to try to do so. The difference now is that I am aware of what I am feeling, and I know the best ways for me to move through it.

Over the years, the triggers stayed the same when holidays and special occasions came around, like First Holy Communions and Confirmations, kindergarten and 8th grade graduations, and my own master's graduation, to name a few. Everyone lines up for the family photos, and a quick sting runs through me, and then I usually reset and try to adjust my focus to the celebration at hand, and all of the wonderful family members that do surround us. In fact, I am often the one insisting on taking photos of everyone, because I know how important it is to capture the memories.

Sometimes I am triggered when I see people who look to be around the age Brian would be today, celebrating great jobs, traveling to cool places, getting engaged, and having babies. If only he could have held on a little longer, maybe he could have experienced these things too. In February of 2024, we rented a mountain house for the weekend in upstate New York with Brendan, Amy, their sweet baby boy, Brendan and all of our pups. As we were driving up to the house, I had this vivid image of Brian with his imagined family joining us too and all the fun we would have together. It just kind of washed over me and I wished so badly that he was there with us.

Triggers can easily be identified by a physical sensation we feel in our body before our brain even realizes what is happening. Maybe it's a knot in our stomach, sweaty palms, hot head, racing heart, or a lump in our throat. Once we know the physical reaction our triggers ignite, we can help ourselves move through tough moments. Mine is usually knots in my stomach and a lump in my throat. Sometimes it is so intense, it feels like the wind got knocked out of me and I can hardly breathe. Other times, I am mad and frustrated, like the feeling right after you stub your toe. And then, sometimes, it is subtle and gentle, but it's there, I just know it's there.

It's hard to avoid triggers because they often catch us off guard, but we can try to reduce the intensity and duration. They can bring us to tears amidst an otherwise okay day or throw us into a complete tailspin. Maybe it's a song on the radio, a smell, a favorite food, a holiday decoration or tradition, even a well-intended comment by a family member or friend. In those moments, I know that I need to come back to the present moment, so that I do not allow my thoughts to get lost in the past, or jump to the future. The best thing we can do is to acknowledge it in the moment. I acknowledge that my heart hurts and that I have permission to feel sad at that time. Sometimes I place both hands over my heart and whisper a simple, *I love you,* or *I miss you*, or *please help me, this is really hard.* Then I take a deep, cleansing breath and try to move on. Ignoring it does not make it go away and acknowledging it feels like a nod of love, and in a way, it makes me feel more connected. Sometimes I am more successful than others, so when it feels like it's too much, I give myself some grace for an extra hard moment. And if I know I am going into a situation where I will likely feel triggered, I try to prepare myself as best as possible with a considerable dose of self-compassion.

The opposite of a trigger is a glimmer, and I absolutely love these! My girlfriend Meg and I share glimmers back and forth regularly. It is our little way of saying hi and sharing something to make the other one smile. Glimmers are those little feelings that make you smile and actually feel good from the inside out. Some of my favorite glimmers include, the sun (literally anything to do with the sun hitting my body, whether I'm outside, on the beach (ideal), or in my car in the winter and the sun warms right through like a greenhouse effect), the smell of coffee brewing, the way Triton snuggles his head in my lap to get as close as possible, when Emily brushes my hair, when Shane discreetly checks on me ("Mom, are you okay?"), when Jay hugs me long enough to make me forget about the rest of the world, a cold IPA, the salty smell of the ocean, blasting music (which genre greatly varies on my mood), dancing (I love to dance), an unexpected text from a friend, tulips, cards with a handwritten note, belly laughs, pizza, sunsets, a perfect avocado, candles, a great glass of red wine, a cozy fireplace, getting lost in a book . . . the list goes on and on.

Can you think of a few? The idea is that when we open ourselves to the abundance of glimmers all around us, glimmers become more visible. Our energy shifts and the good days feel great, and the crappy ones aren't so bad after all. Life is hard when you carry grief, and as you've probably discovered, grief is with us for the long haul. This is precisely why we need to make the best of the days we have. We owe it to ourselves and our loved ones on Earth and beyond to become the best version of ourselves. I am positive that when we stop focusing so much on the people, places, or things that bring us down, and start focusing on the good that surrounds us, we can become happier. It is as if you can change the lens you view life through, because when life gets blurry, we do need to change focus. It's not foolproof, but it works most of the time. It takes consistent effort to become a daily habit, but I'll always try, because neither joy nor sorrow lasts forever, and if another day is not coming, I want to enjoy today.

In a recent training I virtually attended, renowned grief expert, David Kessler, referred to grief bursts and love bursts. A grief burst is a flood of emotions that can come on suddenly and rather intensely. It seems to explain the overwhelming triggering sensations we feel in grief. When we are flooded so deeply it can almost feel like a panic attack or an unexplained sudden illness. We could be in the middle of an ordinary moment when it hits, and then it feels like we need to run and hide immediately. Although seeing three generations of women together still impacts me, sometimes more than others, that first time I saw it I was hit hard. I think that one was more of a grief burst. I share this because I want to normalize the feelings you may be experiencing. I want you to know that these intense, seemingly out of nowhere experiences do not mean you are crazy, they mean you are grieving. The more we can normalize the intense range of emotions that grief so generously pours all over us, the more we can comfort ourselves in even the darkest times.

Like a glimmer, a love burst is a warm and comforting feeling about your loved one, which can also come on suddenly and feel intense. Love bursts will begin to emerge more frequently when you transition out of deep pain and longing into something that feels safer. For instance, when I hear The Beach Boys out of the blue, I always feel an immediate love burst for my mom. I take that moment to honor the emotions rushing through me and thank her for the "Hello." When you are in the store and you see a favorite item of your loved one, you may feel overcome with emotions. This takes time, and in the beginning years a love burst may feel more like a grief burst. Be patient with your process as you begin to take notice of triggers and glimmers and grief bursts and love bursts. Pay attention to how your body is absorbing and reacting to the world around you, and always offer yourself the love and compassion you need in that moment.

Reflection

Where and how do you physically experience triggers in your body?

What, if anything, can you identify specifically that is triggering for you?

What are some of your favorite glimmers? Take the time to really think about these, and as you notice more throughout the day, return to this list and add them.

CHAPTER TEN

healing from the inside out

"To feel too much is dangerous, and to feel too little is tragic."
—David Kessler

When your passion and purpose align with your values, you become unstoppable. What does this mean? Take a moment to think about the things you value most. Maybe it's family, faith, free time, loyalty, humor, financial freedom, health and fitness, this list could go on and on, and everyone's list will be different. Try to focus on your top five values.

Now, are your daily actions aligning with these values? Are you saying this, and doing this? Or are you saying this, but doing that? If you say you value health and fitness, but you haven't worked out in five years, you're out of alignment. If you say you value free time and family time, yet you continue to work yourself into the ground with no end in sight, you are out of alignment. I'm not suggesting you quit your job, I understand that we all have financial responsibilities, but I am suggesting that you acknowledge this, then determine how you can more closely align those actions and values, even if it takes a little while and some creative planning. When we are experiencing grief, the lines can become even more difficult to see. However, it is in this practice of aligning your values and actions when your best self emerges, and you become the person you want to be for yourself and for those around you.

Often this will require you to get a little uncomfortable, to discover who you really want to be at this stage of your life. If we are truly living to our fullest potential, being a student of life and yearning to grow and evolve, it can be a lifelong effort. There is no timeline, if you have breath, you have life and if you have life, you deserve to be living! True growth occurs outside of your comfort zone. Cliche? Absolutely. But also 100% truth. When you are out of alignment, it is important to assess what factors are contributing to this and what you can do to make a change. It's not only okay to make changes in life, but at times essential for your survival. Maybe you did not want this change, but your grief has forced it upon you. It's amazing what we can discover about ourselves when we are faced with the greatest challenges and heartache.

It is necessary to be intentional in your self-discovery because when your goals and your *why* are aligning, then you will discover the *how*. It's easy to get caught up envisioning how it will all work, and sometimes that can become so overwhelming that we give up on something before we even try. It's rare that something so worthwhile comes along with ease. In all honesty, I am glad that I did not realize how much time and energy going back to school would take for me at that stage of my life. If I had, I probably wouldn't have gone through with it. I would have let my guilt consume me, knowing that I was taking too much time from my family. I embraced that process bit by bit and accomplished something I wouldn't have thought possible. Now, being fully immersed in my career, I know that the challenges my own struggles brought me help me have a deeper understanding of other people's struggles and uncertainties and reservations. Even though our circumstances may vary greatly, at the core, we are all seeking very similar things.

When I began my deep dive into personal growth and development, I had no idea how far it would take me. I slowly began consuming content from classics like *The Alchemist* and *To Kill a Mockingbird.* I felt a strong desire to expand my knowledge and my personal literary library, and these two became instant favorites. Then I began moving towards more contemporary self-help books like Glennon Doyle's *Untamed*, Jay Shetty's *Think Like a Monk*, Oprah's *The Path Made Clear* and Edith Eger's, *The Choice*, and anything and everything by Brené Brown, to name just a few. I began to crave this type of content because I was so inspired by the messages. They gave me something outside of my grief to hold on to, and I found it to be deeply motivating. Each message was empowering, encouraging, and unknowingly guiding me on my journey.

Along my educational journey, I was drawn to the ways of various pioneers in the field of psychotherapy and academics including Carl Rogers, Irvin Yalom, Dick Schwartz, Bessel van der Kolk, Dr. Becky Kennedy and David Kessler.

Carl Rogers introduced me to person-centered therapy and the concept of unconditional positive regard, which is a key component in my own practice today. Unconditional positive regard is the basic support and acceptance of another person regardless of their thoughts or behaviors. It is the ability to see a person for who they truly are without judgement. I seek to find the good in everyone and sometimes it is masked by great pain and suffering. In my office, this is so important as many people feel shame or blame themselves for the way things are, and this method allows me to support without being conditional and opens the door for the therapeutic work to take place.

Dr. Schwartz is the founder of Internal Family Systems (IFS), a form of therapy that resonates with me. I have consumed his books, podcasts and educational trainings, and I will continue to learn how to best integrate this approach into my practice. The concept echoed in his many books, including *No Bad Parts,* demonstrates the need to be curious with all of our parts. We can often say things like "If I could just get rid of jealousy or anxiety, then I would be fine" but the truth is that there really are "no bad parts." Because even the parts that at times are seemingly difficult to deal with often show up simply trying to protect us from a perceived threat. When we engage with these parts from a place of curiosity and compassion, we often find that these protective parts are doing their job, or at least what they believe it to be. Maybe as a child we needed certain parts to respond in a way of protection, but as adults, we have the capability of handling things in a more regulated manner. The more in tune we become to our parts, the better we can manage challenging situations and avoid or reduce highly heightened states.

Dr. Becky Kennedy is a phenomenon. Parenting is hard, and as her famous book, *Good Inside*, reminds us, we are all good at our core, parents and children alike, even when we are struggling. She shares the need to be sturdy and compassionate with our children, while building stronger bonds and helping children develop resilience. By validating our children's emotions, we are cultivating more emotionally secure individuals. And as parents, we too, have the responsibility to model that same behavior we wish to see in our children. Dr. Becky reminds us that while all feelings are welcome, all behaviors are not. I highly recommend Dr. Becky to parents that come through my office seeking more support, especially her succinct Instagram reels, which have helped me numerous times.

In 1969, Dr. Elisabeth Kübler-Ross introduced the "5 Stages of Grief", which included denial, anger, bargaining, depression, and acceptance. It is important to note that these stages are not linear, and obviously neither is grief. Grief is messy and confusing and constantly fluctuating. In fact, the one certainty with grief is that it will continue to change. In 2019, world renowned grief expert,

David Kessler, introduced the "The Sixth Stage of Grief" in his book, *Finding Meaning*. "Finding meaning" does not justify a loss, it refers to transforming grief into a more meaningful and peaceful experience, by finding ways of honoring our loved one's memory. This sixth step is not one that you can expect to step into immediately, but over time, this can become the most important part of healing in your grief journey.

I began to learn quickly that I would only be able to go as far with my clients as I was willing to go with myself if I wanted to be a good counselor. I did not go back to school at this stage in my life to just be mediocre. The call on my heart to sit with others through their pain and challenges was so strong that I knew my personal work needed to be done from the inside out. I never thought that I wasn't facing my pain along the way, but I also did not realize how much I was avoiding. It was not and has not been easy. I say this because grief is a constant recurrence in my life. Everything can feel just fine . . . and then it strikes me, and I know at that point I need to acknowledge it, lean in, and work through it.

Going back to school tore back the curtain and made it very clear that I still had a lot of work to do. Pursuing a master's degree in counseling continually required me to reflect and become more self-aware. Writing this book also made me more aware of my relationship with my personal grief. At one point early in 2024, many clients on my caseload were seeking therapy for grief support. It became so overwhelming that Sonora asked one day, only half seriously, "Should we put Grief Therapist over your door?" While I'm not at the point where I only want to see people who are moving through grief, I had a big internal *Ah-ha* moment when I finally knew *why* I wrote this book. Writing this book has been incredibly painful at times, some days I would cry so hard, while recounting such horrible memories, I just did not think I had it in me and I wanted to throw in the towel. I would continually ask, *why am I doing this to myself?* But I realized that processing and reprocessing my own grief has allowed me to be more fully present and engaged with my clients. It also does not mean that it is not extremely sad at times, I have certainly shed many tears with clients. However, I am shedding tears in that moment for their loss, not mine, and being able to separate that was, and is, absolutely necessary. In a virtual training I attended with David Kessler, he said, "Grief work is not necessarily work we choose, it chooses you." I strongly concur.

Fear held me back from so many things for such a long time: fear of failure, fear of the unknown, fear of discovering my true potential, or lack thereof. When I embraced fear head on, I didn't just explore a new career path, I also faced many more fears. I learned how to ski at 42. There were many years of struggling, being so afraid of getting hurt, being stuck on the bunny slope while my family cruised the mountain because I sent them away, cursing and crying and incredibly frustrated. I realized that fear was making me tense and keeping me stuck. I eventually embraced a new mindset with determination, and it finally clicked. Now, I am not gracefully flying down black diamonds, but I am slow and steady on a green mountain and sometimes even a blue and can usually successfully get off the ski lift. Oh, and I'm writing a book today! Take that, fear.

In the early months of 2025, I came across a trend on Instagram called "I met my younger self for coffee". The trend was inspired by poet and author, Jennae Cecelia, from her latest book *Deep in My Feels.* I began to read dozens of these letters people wrote to their younger selves and could not stop the tears from flowing. Becoming so consumed with the content, I decided to make a coffee date with my 17-year-old self. If this exercise resonates with you, I strongly encourage you to also write a letter to your younger self, at whichever age comes to your mind.

I met my younger self for coffee . . .

We both arrived on time and appeared more than a little anxious

She ordered her coffee light and sweet, I ordered mine black

She was 17, I am 43

Her eyes smiled at me with wondering awe, mine smiled back with a mixture of heartache and pain knowing what she has yet to endure . . . and an unimaginable joy for the family she has yet to create

She shared her hopes and dreams, I told her they would all come true, just not at all how she imagined

She glanced at my wedding rings and shared her heartache of love gone wrong, I told her that nothing is wasted and that her greatest love story was coming soon

She shared the chaos of a crazy house with two parents, five kids and two dogs,

and I told her she has no idea how much she will miss that chaos, and in that moment I ached to live just one more day there

I told her I was ***really proud of her****, I told her there were going to be some impossible days in her future and that through the grace of God, she would find the strength to get through the darkest nights and the most tumultuous storms. I told her she won't do it alone.*

I told her that she will still dance in the kitchen and sing loudly in the car

I told her we still cry at everything, but our sensitivity has come to serve us well

I told her that our daughter is beautiful and smart and quick witted and way cooler than we ever were . . . I told her that our son is so handsome and also so much smarter than we ever were and that when he smiles, we smile, every. single. time.

I told her we married a cute surfer boy and that he is honest and loyal and hardworking, and fun and patient and loving, and that he is by far the best friend we've ever had and that sometimes we too, dance in the kitchen

I told her the call on her heart to do something different with her career will not stop until she makes the move. I told her every experience she has is preparing her for this and that when the time is just right, she will know exactly what she needs to do

I told her we now spend our days listening, supporting, encouraging and teaching others the tools to get through the dark days and it is the most rewarding and mutually healing profession

I told her we embrace gratitude as a way of living with a heart full of appreciation for all the things

I told her to trust herself, even when it seems scary

I told her that Mommy was right, "Faith is our greatest tool" and that she will rely on it heavily

When it was time to go, neither of us wanted to leave or end our hug first, our eyes filled with tears

I told her "I love you" and one day she will understand this and believe it too as I squeezed her one last time

This is your not-so-gentle reminder that it is NOT TOO LATE! It is never too late to pursue what makes you come alive. I assure you that as you prepare to take your last breath, you will never regret the times you took chances on yourself, but you will absolutely regret the ones you never took because you made excuses or you succumbed to fear. The little things are the big things nudging you along the way.

When I've had the privilege to work with clients who are nearing the last stage of their lives, or family members who have had to say goodbye, this concept is something that is clear to them. Don't wait. Don't waste time holding on to grudges or telling yourself you can't. I am here to say, yes you can, and, with certainty, your life will improve. So, make the phone call, take the trip, go back to school, write the book, and whatever you do, pour everything you've got into it. Do not just live through your pain, GROW through your pain.

I know that I still don't have it all figured out, and I never will. But I will never stop exploring and learning and pushing myself. It is in this way that my imposter syndrome significantly decreased shortly after beginning my new career. I realized that when the door closed, and it was me and another person, I was locked in that moment. I focus on the person in front of me, with anxiety or depression or marital struggles, or baby blues or grief. I know that I can sit still with them because I have been healing these parts of me. I can show them the way, and when they are willing to do the work, it is always worth it. My job is a different kind of hard some days, and my tiredness is an emotional exhaustion most days, but it is beyond rewarding to hold space and see signs of healing peeping through.

It is important that you have self-compassion as you ease yourself back into your life following a grief-inducing experience. Dr. Kristin Neff, a top expert in this field, explains that self-compassion is the process of turning compassion inward. This can be tricky, especially when we feel lost and alone in our grief. I remember specific instances after each of my major losses where I found myself utterly distraught, thinking about the life I once knew. My once very bubbly social battery drained so easily. I have come to recognize the people I surround myself with who increase my energy levels and provide a social gain, and I have noticed where I am depleted and experience the social drain. Sometimes it has to do with a particular day I may be experiencing, and sometimes it is just the way our energy interacts with others. The more aware we can become, the better we can support ourselves in our grief and beyond. We can do this by setting boundaries for ourselves, anticipating, and preparing. The relationships in your life, and the people who you surround yourself with, are so impactful to your peace. Choose, whenever possible, to spend time with the people who recharge your soul.

The summer after my mom died, my childhood friend Kristin had a party at her house. We had been close friends since elementary school and have remained friends to this day. Everyone was home from college for the summer, and it was the first time most people had connected since Christmas break. I was looking forward to seeing my friends, but I was also really nervous. Some of them I hadn't seen since the funeral, others I hadn't seen at all since my mom died. Although anxious, I didn't anticipate just how emotional I would be. I remember spending most of the night inside talking with a couple of friends and crying. Just thinking about that night, I am flooded with emotions. Mommy had this incredible way of making everyone feel loved. Oftentimes friends would come to my house, and I wouldn't even know that they were there because they had been sitting and chatting with my mom, venting about a boyfriend or something else going on in their lives. My mom would comfort them, encourage them, and support them. Everyone always said how loved they felt by her and how she could make them feel so much better in just a few moments, especially with one of her big, strong hugs. So that night when my friends saw me, it reminded them that she was gone. It was hard and there was mutual sadness. They missed her too and they were sad for me and my family. While the tears were heavy, I also felt comforted, and I was grateful to be surrounded by so much love. It breaks my heart that the close friends I made later in life will never get to have those special moments with my mom.

After Brian died, I remember feeling the same way. I just wanted to hide. I didn't feel like I could be myself around anyone. I honestly felt dead inside for a while. I didn't want to fake it all the time, but my best friends were so patient with me. I remember a night a few weeks after Brian died when we took the kids out for a boat ride and met up with our friends Lauren and Doug. Their son,

Zack, and Emily had been besties since they were in our bellies. It was such a beautiful night on the water, light winds, a big, bright moon illuminating the sky, and that salty bay smell hung in the air. I forced myself to go that night, even though I was hurting so deeply, I knew that I would be in good company. By the end of the night, I was laughing through tears watching the kids being silly, trying to hold on to a bit of normal, even if for just a moment, and it made me feel so loved.

A few months later, we went away over the new year to the mountains with Michelle and Nick and their boys, Landen and Malcolm. For the first few days I was hanging in there, but on New Year's Eve I completely fell apart. How could I end this year without my brother? How could I start a new year that he didn't live in? It was all too much, and my feelings were washing over me like a tsunami. And yet once again, I leaned into the comfort of my friends and felt so loved and safe in that moment. It would be a long time before I could embrace being in big crowds and feeling like myself again, but in those early months, being with friends who were truly like family, who treated my children as their own, who seemed to know what I needed before I even knew, those are the things I'll never forget.

Shortly after my dad died, my cousins Tom and Andy lost their parents almost a year apart from one another. My Uncle Tom was my mom's cousin, and they had shared many adventurous stories of growing up together in New York. In the early 1990's, Uncle Tom's work was relocated to New Jersey. My mom and Uncle Tom were thrilled to be together again and have this chance to raise their kids together. Tommy and Andy were a few years younger than me and matched up just right with Brendan and Brian. Together the four of them were trouble, and it was wonderful. They found their own kind of brotherhood and the next generation of cousins began.

Brian's death took a big toll on them as well. They felt the same enormous loss and sense of helplessness we were experiencing.

Then their lives took an even greater turn in 2019 when Uncle Tom passed suddenly. He had a larger-than-life personality, and his loss was devastating. And then in 2020, before the pandemic started, Tommy and Andy's mom, Aunt Chris, passed after a courageous battle with Multiple Sclerosis. Aunt Chris was kind and warm and managed through her debilitating condition with grace. Our cousins became parentless adults like us, in less than a year, and we felt that mutual pain. Together with their supportive wives, they pushed through too. Andy's wife Meg was always such a wonderful caretaker to her mother-in-law as her MS progressed, and the way she treated her as her own is etched in my heart. I always admired her for that, among other things. Tommy truly strives to keep his parents, our parents and Brian alive in spirit. He never misses an anniversary or special occasion to reach out to let me, and my siblings know that we are on his mind. The way he walks through his grief inspires me and lifts me up on days I need a boost. I feel so grateful for the closeness our parents cultivated that we will carry on forever.

Over the years, I have seen my nephews Michael and Owen, and my niece Morgan, creating memories and traditions with Shane and Emily, and it truly warms my heart. The five of them have a very close-knit bond. When we have nearly 30 people squeezed in our house for Thanksgiving, almost half being kids, I see the joy and connection through all of them, just like we had many years ago. I know that my children and my nieces and nephews are absorbing the traditions, and energetic love is being stored in their hearts and minds.

There are so many ways we can offer help to others in grief. People often will not know what they need during this time, maybe you can relate. For instance, if you say, "let me know if you need anything," they likely will not ask, not because they don't want help, but they really don't know what they need. The most important way to offer support is to "hold space". Maybe you are wondering, what does "hold space" even mean? Let them tell you the story of how their loved one died, or maybe a silly memory of when they were alive, even if it is repeated several times. You are not reminding someone that their loved one died by bringing it up, you are remembering that they lived. Our love for those we love does not end in death, it stays with us. Allowing someone to share stories of their loved one, or simply allowing them to cry, is a powerful form of friendship. We also can step in to do things without being asked, such as prepare a meal, arrange a ride for their child, set up a cleaning service, drop off their favorite sweet treat or join them for a walk and talk.

Over the past two decades, I have also expanded my frame of reference. My viewpoint is not the only one. It is very clear to me that my siblings have all experienced these losses in unique ways. When I try to put myself in their shoes for a moment, I can see glimpses of how their lives were impacted and the choices they made as a result. I believe through it all, we all did the very best we could at the time, even Brian. Our struggles still find us, and we rely on each other, our spouses, our children and the individual coping skills we have all developed over the years to get us through those extra hard moments.

My friends have also played a major role in my healing journey over the years. Michelle and Lauren have shown up time and time again. Through our family adventures of travel, celebrating religious and educational milestones together for our children, and the day to day of raising families together, they have both offered selfless and unconditional friendship and love. My girlfriend Tiffany remembers every anniversary and sends a text before I even open my eyes. She also always knows when to check in and circle back around, just to make sure I am okay. Her intentions are always so genuine and comforting. Marybeth reminisces with me about our younger years. We share memories of my mom, and all our silly antics, what we tried to get away with as teens and still wondering how we both had so many chores. When we get together, even if it has been months since we last saw each other, it always feels like no time has passed at all. Emily reminds me of moments with my mom that still make her heart smile, and she reminds me of a simpler time before the world changed forever, when we were just best friends living our best, care-free lives. We both feel immensely grateful for the friendship our mothers initiated and know in our hearts that we are forever connected. Joneil always makes me laugh and reminds me not to take myself so seriously all the time. Tara shares her strong faith and offers insight and comfort during many of my emotional venting sessions. Beth is always available to talk through a wishing our moms were still here for this kind of moment, a teen parenting dilemma or to simply offer love and support for the craziness that is our 40's. My girlfriend Megan sends the most thoughtful gifts that speak directly to my heart. Gifting is her love language, and she shares it generously. She opened her first garden and gift shop, *Vine,* in the fall of 2024 and it is like walking into her soul; talk about connecting to your purpose! When my girlfriend Christi lost her dad after a brutally long battle with Parkinson's, which happened to be on the same day of my mom's anniversary, we knew our shared day would forever connect our hearts to each other. We also connect deeply through our strong faith.

After each loss, I initially resisted seeking out my friends for support. I only wanted to be with my family or alone. The thing is, we are not meant to do this alone, and in time, I came to need those friendships again. I also needed to release the guilt of having a happy moment. How could I have fun when they are gone? It's such a complicated feeling, but one that anyone who has experienced significant loss can relate to. It just feels wrong on some level. But I have come to realize that not only is it wrong to *block* joy, but it is also necessary to *seek* joy. And I am often reminded that neither joy nor sorrow lasts forever, so now when I am feeling joyful with friends, I try to be all in because I know all too well that sorrow will find me again, and when it does, I will remind myself that it also will not last forever.

Don't wait to take control of your own life. Nobody's coming to save you, and nobody is doing this work for you. You need to do this for yourself; *it's time to choose you.* My thing is likely not your thing. It's okay to change your course to find what sets your soul on fire. And when you continue to get warmer, you know you are getting close to the flame. Keep searching for your flame, search for the deeper purpose layered within the pain. It may evolve, but the key is, don't ever stop. There is no end to this journey of self-growth and discovery. Let that fire glow and spread the light of your flame all around you. Hold your torch high, **be a light** for yourself, *and* for others.

If you don't know what your thing is, that is okay too. It's not always easy to see, and most of us don't know what we want to do with our lives when we are 18, 45 or even 70! Meet yourself exactly where you are right at this moment. I saw a quote online from an unknown author that said "You're not healing to be able to handle trauma, pain, anxiety, depression. You're used to those. You're healing to be able to handle joy and accept happiness back into your life." Yes, exactly that.

Ask the people who love you the most what they think are your greatest strengths. See if there are any overlaps in what you think your own strengths are, then dig a little deeper. Do you believe them? Do you agree? When do you feel like you come alive? This exercise is not pompous or self-indulgent, this is part of the discovery process. Allow yourself to be a beginner, allow yourself to be humbled by the process, and then try again. Eventually you will realize which strengths set you apart. Ten people can do the same job, but they all bring a completely different vibe and energy. What is your energy? What is the call on your heart? I implore you to find it, to channel your grief into something that fuels you and lights you up because I promise that when you figure it out, everything will change for the better. As the great Paulo Coelho said in *The Alchemist*, "When you want something, all the universe conspires in helping you to achieve it."

Gratitude is the biggest muscle you can exercise every day and continue to receive major rewards. When you start to be truly thankful in your heart, good things get bigger and multiply exponentially. Yes, there will still be pain and heartache along the way, none of us are immune to the human experience. But what if the days that were okay could be great? When the alarm clock is blaring in the morning, do you roll over, hit snooze, then start complaining about not wanting to get up? And then maybe you hit snooze again, dreading work, complaining all the way to the bathroom about the day ahead. What if instead, when the alarm clock goes off, you say, *Thank you for this day. Thank you for my family. Thank you for the sunshine. Thank you for the comfy blanket and pillows.* That's how I start my day now. Before I get out of bed I finish with my mantra, *help me help others, help me help myself.* It takes less than a minute. Then I walk to the bathroom with a few more thank you's in my head. Positive affirmations and positive self-talk boost dopamine receptors from a neuroscience perspective. They are actually very good for us. Give it a try and see how different the tone of your day feels.

This is not a new concept, but sometimes it makes a difference when you receive the message, and if the timing is right, it just sticks. An article written by Amanda Logan, APRN, C.N.P., Primary Care, Family Medicine, on the *Mayo Clinic Health System* website stated, "Expressing gratitude is associated with a host of mental and physical benefits. Studies have shown that feeling thankful can improve sleep, mood and immunity. Gratitude can decrease depression, anxiety, difficulties with chronic pain and risk of disease."

Another article entitled *The Neuroscience of Gratitude and Effects on the Brain,* found on PositivePsychology.com and written by Madhuleena Roy Chowdhury, BA, shared the following about gratitude, "It produces a feeling of long-lasting happiness and contentment, the physiological basis of which lies at the neurotransmitter level. When we express gratitude and receive the same, our brain releases dopamine and serotonin, the two crucial neurotransmitters responsible for our emotions, and they make us feel 'good'. They enhance our mood immediately, making us feel happy from the inside. By consciously practicing gratitude every day, we can help these neural pathways to strengthen themselves and ultimately create a permanent grateful and positive nature within ourselves."

I have not done this forever. I heard about gratitude long before I really understood it, and certainly long before I started making it a daily practice. It's not just something nice we say or a list we make at Thanksgiving. It is a daily practice of recognizing the blessings that surround us and keeping our focus on that. The view is much more beautiful than focusing on the hurt and the pain and suffering. I know, because I did that for too long.

I know that every season of life hits differently, and maybe in this particular season, saying thank you feels too hard. Maybe it feels fake because life has been so hard and you just don't want to say it, I get it. But when you are having a slightly better day, try it. Or maybe just try to notice simple things that feel good throughout the day, the first sip of coffee or the sun warming your skin.

When you are feeling too overwhelmed to even say thank you, focus on the basics. When we are steeped in grief, the most basic human needs can be neglected. If this is where you are right now, ask yourself these questions daily. Did I eat today? Did I drink enough water? When was the last time I showered? Everyone's grief journey will look different. Take as much time as you need and when you are ready, try to slowly pepper in gratitude.

Our grief is not meant to be bottled up and shoved down deep inside. Our grief is meant to be expressed. Our grief is meant to be shared in the sacred space of others who can hold our tears and our memories with tender, loving care. In doing so, we give permission to others to feel safe enough to share their own grief too. When we connect with our grief and others, it is a spiritual act, and although our tears may flow, somehow our hearts can feel lighter in those moments and the burden we carry lessens ever so slightly. Every time we slow down to feel the grief, we are contributing to our own healing.

My grief has allowed me insight that I can confidently say I would not have had otherwise. I do not believe there is a reason for a particular death, nor do I search for a silver lining, it simply does not exist. I would not choose these experiences if given the choice, but I have chosen to allow the grief to transform me, and I have recognized how to learn and grow from it. Being able to connect intimately with others is incredibly rewarding. I can sit down and scan a room and take a moment to honor each person around me and send them love, because every single person around you is going through something. Hence came the origin of the word "sonder." Sonder was coined by writer John Koenig around 2012, in his blog *The Dictionary of Obscure Sorrows* (published as a print book in 2021). Koenig defines the word as "the realization that each random passerby is living a life as vivid and complex as your own." In grief, we can innocently be so consumed with our own sorrow that we forget others are still going through their own experiences, challenges and struggles. I have certainly been guilty of this in the past, and make a conscious effort now to be more considerate and aware.

I would be remiss to say that there are no comparisons here. I haven't experienced the worst. In my opinion, there could be nothing greater than the loss of a child . . . and yet I also do not diminish my losses. Grief would be an ugly competition, and honestly a battle I would not want to win. Regardless, I chose to share my story because of the relentless calling on my soul to do so. Because maybe, just maybe, someone will come across it at a critical time when despair is their only language. Maybe something about my story will provide comfort and hope to a grieving mother, father, sister, brother, husband, wife, aunt, uncle, best friend, coach, teacher or coworker. Maybe, just maybe, it will help one person get through a dark day, and that is why I chose to share this story of my intimate 25+ year relationship with grief.

While writing this book, one of my clients died after a courageous battle with cancer, leaving behind her young children. My friend whom I write about in this book, Erin Ryan, lost her battle to a viciously aggressive cancer. A former classmate of Shane's lost her heroic battle to a rare cancer and her family aches in her absence. Another friend had to say goodbye to her father after years of being the go-to caregiver, and another friend had to say goodbye to her brother. Another friend said goodbye to her mother, and I wept with her. Numerous clients of mine have lost children, spouses, parents, and close friends. I'm not mentioning this so you can compare or compete with their grief, the purpose is simply to demonstrate that grief never really ends. And yet, there is still *life after death*.

Now it's your turn. Taking even the smallest step forward is still taking a step. In the quiet of your heart and your mind, take the hand of that small child inside of you. Let them know that the pain is not gone, but it is time to bravely carry on. Love yourself fiercely through this process and allow for unlimited grace and self-compassion. Talk to yourself with the support and encouragement you would give to your oldest and dearest friend. Allow me to join you on your path if you need some company. Borrow my emotional support comfort blanket, and then when you feel ready, share it with a friend. There can be tremendous healing when we not only embrace our pain, but we also allow the pain to transform into the most beautiful form of unconditional and everlasting love.

Reflection

What do you value most? Use the list below to highlight your most important core values. This list is not comprehensive. Feel free to add your own if something is missing for you.

Acceptance
Achievement
Adventure
Authenticity
Beauty
Balance
Bravery
Clarity
Community
Creativity
Curiosity
Diversity
Empathy
Enthusiasm
Ethics
Faith
Family
Fitness
Freedom
Fulfillment
Fun
Generosity
Gratitude
Grit
Health
Humor
Independence
Integrity
Intelligence
Intimacy
Kindness
Joy
Leadership
Learning
Loyalty
Mindfulness
Personal Growth
Partnership
Playfulness
Popularity
Power
Resilience
Respect
Safety
Security
Self-Expression

Service
Simplicity
Solitude
Spirituality
Teamwork
Trustworthiness
Usefulness
Expertise
Warmth
Wisdom
Vitality

Are your actions today aligning with your values? If not, how can you change this? Remember, even small steps count!

What are your greatest strengths? Not sure? If this question is hard for you, what do the people you love think are your greatest strengths? Ask them, and then maybe you can share what you think theirs are too.

Take some time to develop your gratitude list. When you are finished, take a picture and revisit this list whenever life feels extra hard and you need to be reminded. Use these images as anchor thoughts whenever you need an emotional redirection. You can come back and add to this as often as you would like. Remember, when we start focusing on the good around us, it grows.

Breathwork and Grounding Exercises

The following are a few therapeutic techniques I use in my office regularly. You can do these exercises anywhere, at any time. These mindfulness exercises allow you to focus on the present moment and create calm in your body. As oxygen pumps and your heart rate slows, you will start to feel more relaxed. Utilizing a breathing exercise can help you get through a triggering or grief fueled moment.

If it feels right for you when you achieve your calm, you can also use that moment to set an intention. Intentions can vary greatly, some may include, healing, letting go, clarity, peace, and self-compassion, to name a few, or perhaps you are offering your intention to someone who can use the positive energy. Choose whatever intention comes to your mind.

Try the following exercises and see what feels most comfortable for you. It is important to practice these techniques regularly so that when you are in a difficult or anxiety-induced situation you are comfortable using them to calm yourself.

The Power of the Pause

When we take a moment to pause, and breathe, using one of these strategies below, we allow ourselves the chance to *respond* instead of *reacting* in any situation, which leads to more considerate communication towards ourselves and others.

The Stop Sign

This visual strategy can be used to redirect our thoughts when they become intrusive or overwhelming. Imagine a big, red stop sign in front of your face and use this image to stop what you are doing and change course. It may help to go for a walk, get a glass of water or wash your hands, or even stick your face in the freezer for a few seconds. It helps to physically do something to distract your mind from unwanted thoughts. Once you have redirected, you can use a breathing technique.

Breathwork

4-7-8

First, we begin with the breath in through the nose, try breathing in for 4 seconds, holding your breath for 7 seconds and then a long, slow release for 8 seconds, out of your mouth AHHHHHH. Repeat this several times until you really get the desired cleansing breath you are trying to achieve. If you notice tension in a particular part of the body, visualize sending extra breath to that area.

Box Breathing

Another powerful breathing exercise is box breathing. For this exercise, imagine drawing a box with your breath. As you draw the top line, breathe in for 4 seconds, then draw a line down and breathe out for 4 seconds, draw another line over and breathe in for 4 seconds, and finally connect the box with the final line and breathe out for 4 seconds. Repeat this a few times.

Grounding of the Senses Technique

Grounding is another way to create calm in your body and your mind. It forces you to think and look around, which allows you to get out of the thought loop you may be stuck in. To practice grounding, you can follow these 5 simple steps.

5. Take notice of **FIVE** things you see around you. It could be your water bottle, a picture on the wall, anything you can see in your surroundings.

4. Take notice of **FOUR** things you can touch around you. It could be your dog, your own body, or the sweater you are wearing, anything you can touch.

3. Take notice of **THREE** things you hear. It could be the ticking of the clock, the text ding on your phone, anything you can hear.

2. Take notice of **TWO** things you can smell. It could be

a candle burning, or perfume, or the smell of something cooking, anything you can smell.

1. Take notice of **ONE** thing you can taste. It could be your last sip of coffee or your lunch, one thing you can taste.

By paying close attention to each of your 5 senses, you can bring your awareness and focus back to the present moment. This is another way to reset yourself and restore a sense of calm in your body.

Anchor Images

Another way to utilize the five senses is to create anchor images for each sense. Trace your hand on a piece of paper, like you would do in elementary school. On each finger, write one of the senses, then go through each and identify a sense that is favorable to you. For example, sense of touch, for me, is petting Triton, I always find that to be extremely soothing and calming. When you have identified each one, close your eyes and clearly envision yourself seeing, tasting, touching, feeling and hearing your favorite things. You can lock these anchor thoughts into your mind and use them as go-to tools when you need a mental shift.

very special thanks . . .

"Nobody knows how to say goodbye" —The Lumineers

From my heart to yours, thank you for taking this journey with me. I hope this book has inspired you to tap deeper into your own purpose and meaning and to notice the significant connections (not coincidences) throughout your own life. There are signs guiding you from everywhere. I hope you know and believe that you are brave enough to embrace them, and you can open yourself to receiving all the good in this life that you wholeheartedly deserve.

XO, *Meaghan*

A thousand thank you's to my husband and best friend, Jason Hughes, *for literally everything. I could not have done this without you. Your support, encouragement, and unwavering faith in my ability to complete this book has been instrumental. I love you so much and am so grateful to have you by my side.* XO

Special thanks to my son, Shane Edward Hughes, *for allowing me to share your personal writing of such a painful memory. Thank you to my daughter,* Emily Joan Hughes, *for your continued encouragement and*

confidence boosts. I am so proud of both of you today and every day and I know that your angels in Heaven are too.

Special thanks to Brian Thomas Brice for all the nudges from up above every time I wanted to throw in the towel and say forget it, it's way too hard and painful, or why am I doing this? I knew it was you pushing me along. Love you forever and always. Thanks for being the "Fire and Flood" (Vance Joy) that I needed to get through this.

Special thanks to my siblings, Kerry, Gail Katherine, and Brendan, for not only allowing me to share this story, but also for encouraging me to do so. Your collective support has been a blessing, and I am so appreciative.

Thank you to Tara Smith for suggesting I connect to Kirsten Flemming. Thank you to Kirsten Flemming for suggesting I connect with Courtney Greenhalgh. Together, you each helped me get to the next step in making this book a reality, and thank you to Courtney Greenhalgh for recommending Mayfly book design and publishing services.

Special thanks to my editor, Courtney Greenhalgh, of dandelion literary services, who saw my vision and encouraged me to run with it. You showed me where I could go deeper and offered continual support and encouragement. So very grateful to have been on this journey with you. Thank you, thank you, thank you!

And last, but not least, a very special thank you to the team at Mayfly, especially Jess LaGreca Steidl and Julie Scheife for helping turn my manuscript into a beautiful book.

suicide resources

If you are thinking about suicide, are worried about a friend or loved one, or are in need of emotional support, the 988 Suicide & Crisis Lifeline is available 24/7 across the United States. Remember, you are not alone, and talking to someone can help save a life.

Please Call or Text 988 or visit
https://988lifeline.org/talk-to-someone-now/

grief resources

If you are interested in continuing your grief healing journey, check out David Kessler's comprehensive and supportive site, ***Grief.com****. You can access more information for the Tender Hearts online grief support community, along with many other valuable resources.*

To get more information about ***Common Ground Grief Center****, or to see how you can help support their foundation, please visit www.commongroundgriefcenter.org/*

Anderson Cooper hosts the Podcast, ***All There Is*** *around his own experiences with grief and opens a conversation with his guests, as they share their grief journeys. It is a beautiful resource that reinforces the universality we experience through grief, while offering comfort and support on a deeper level.*

about the author

Meaghan A. Hughes is a Licensed Professional Counselor, writer, and mother whose work is deeply rooted in her own lived experience with grief, loss, and resilience. Meaghan's own losses led her to pursue a career change and become a mental health professional at the age of 41.

Life After Death is Meaghan's real-life story and debut book. Meaghan lives at the Jersey Shore with her husband, Jason, their two children, Shane and Emily, and their black lab, Triton.

www.ingramcontent.com/pod-product-compliance
Ingram Content Group UK Ltd.
Pitfield, Milton Keynes, MK11 3LW, UK
UKHW042019190726
13854UKWH00005B/2369